WHAT REALLY HAPPENED

WHAT REALLY HAPPENED

*Unexpected Insights From Life's
Uncomfortable Moments*

SHARI CAUDRON

Ghost Road Press

Denver Colorado

Some of the pieces published here originally appeared in *Workforce Magazine*, *The Hindu Sunday Magazine*, and *The Christian Science Monitor*.

Author's Note: I have changed the names of some people in this book so they won't get mad at me.

Library of Congress Cataloging-in-Publication Data.
Caudron, Shari
What Really Happened.

Ghost Road Press
ISBN 0-9760729-1-2 (pbk.)
Library of Congress Control Number: 2005921633

Cover Photo: Gregory O'Toole
Book Design: Jenny Hill
Cover Design: Sonya Unrein

Ghost Road Press
www.ghostroadpress.com

For Allan Halcrow

"The trouble with using experience as a guide is that the final exam often comes before the lesson."
ANONYMOUS

Contents

Foreword　　　　　　　　　　　　　　　　　　10

The Occidental Tourist　　　　　　　　　　　13

Not Just Another Fish Story　　　　　　　　19

Opera for Dummies　　　　　　　　　　　　25

Book Keeping　　　　　　　　　　　　　　33

Talkin' about Chicken　　　　　　　　　　43

Whiners Need Not Apply　　　　　　　　　49

Seek and Ye Shall...Seek　　　　　　　　　53

Thinking The Worst　　　　　　　　　　　71

The Gift of Envy　　　　　　　　　　　　75

Looking For Lacy　　　　　　　　　　　　81

Why We Work　　　　　　　　　　　　　95

Pee Here Now　　　　　　　　　　　　　99

How To Rent A Video　　　　　　　　　105

Time Sharing　　　　　　　　　　　　　111

In Praise of Reunions　　　　　　　　　　123

The Real Digital Divide　　　　　　　　　129

Beat It　　　　　　　　　　　　　　　　135

Avoiding A Hostel Takeover　　　　　　　141

Teaching Lessons　　　　　　　　　　　145

Sawbones　　　　　　　　　　　　　　　155

Restoration Hardware　　　　　　　　　159

Forty-Three Things I Now Do
　　That I'd Never Thought I'd Do　　　　165

I Hereby Resolve　　　　　　　　　　　169

Higher Ground　　　　　　　　　　　　175

FOREWORD

As readers, we look for a writer with whom we can connect. Someone to learn from, to laugh with—a traveling companion who will take us places we haven't been and perhaps can't get to on our own. We also look for writers to whom we can relate—those who have had similar experiences, similar thoughts. The best authors see the hidden ironies in life, the humor in uncomfortable situations. They make us see the fantastic in normal occurrences. And they show us they are just like us—people living with the same aspirations, dreams, and phobias. If they've done their jobs correctly, they can entertain and teach us at the same time, weaving each so seamlessly we haven't even noticed what really happened until the book has been closed.

As a publisher, I am never at a loss for traveling companions. They arrive almost daily, big manilla envelopes piling up on my desk, spilling over to the top of a box that sits on the floor. I eventually read them all, knowing some of the manuscripts will be better than others—and that some will be exceptional. It is the exceptional ones I rely on for return visits, the exceptional ones placed on my bookshelf so I can be rewarded by their proximity.

When I was ten years old, I suffered from a number of phobias that the limbic part of my brain randomly sent my way. Most of these fears would appear from out of the blue, like when I was swimming in the deep end of the neighborhood pool and I suddenly realized I couldn't touch the bottom and I might drown if my feet stopped kicking, or the time I leaned over a second story railing at the local shopping mall and couldn't focus or breathe and knew if I kept looking over the railing, my feet would leave the ground and I would flip over. The ventriloquist horror movie *Magic*, starring a young Anthony Hopkins and a terrifying mannequin, also provoked an irrational limbic phobia I've never shared with anyone and never dreamed anyone else but me had. Then I read Shari Caudron's book.

That's why I so appreciate Shari's writing talent and why when her manuscript arrived in my office, it went right to the special spot on my bookshelf. Because I knew it was the kind of book I wanted to share with readers who are like me.

Shari carries us with her as she chronicles her travels, the exotic trips as well as the daily travails. She allows us to eavesdrop on her conversations with strangers, partners, family, and friends. She helps us see the extraordinary in the ordinary, the eloquence in talking about chicken in a coffee shop, the foolishness of feeling guilty for buying books but never having time to read them. And by the end, we've found a good guide and a good friend.

Isn't that what we, as readers, desire? When I first read these essays you now hold in your hands, I felt an automatic rapport with their author, a distinct sense of ease. I knew I had found someone I could hang out with, laugh with. Someone who isn't afraid to show her shortcomings and in turn, show me mine. It's the gifted writers who can do this and not seem pretentious, and it's what Shari does best.

Now it's time to introduce you to Shari Caudron. It won't take long to get to know her, just a sentence or two and you'll feel her warmth and insight. I'm confident when you've reached the last page, you'll feel you've also found a companion with whom you'll want to travel again. I know I have.

—Matthew Davis, Editor

THE OCCIDENTAL TOURIST

It's 1:30 on an overcast May afternoon and I'm standing in front of a guest cabin on the Victoria Princess, a small cruise ship traveling down the Yangtze River in Southern China. I'm pretty sure this is the massage room, and I'm fairly certain I managed to schedule an appointment. Still, I hesitate before knocking.

A petite woman in white silk pajamas and straight black bangs opens the door. She is half my size, half my age, and twice as beautiful. Not that I'm beautiful but, well, you get the idea. Standing next to her I feel large, pink, and hairy. She points to the massage table, looks up at me, and raises an eyebrow. Oh. It must be time to undress. I wait for her to leave but she merely crosses her arms and steps to the side.

As I undress I watch a barge drift by the uncurtained window. On its deck, workmen in green rain slickers heave boxes and coil rope. They try not to look in the window; I try not to look outside. It dawns on me that the Chinese, who share tiny apartments with large extended families, have a very different concept of modesty than I do.

Once naked, I begin to slide under the sheet on the massage table and the small, now-frowning woman rushes up, grabs the sheet with both hands, and gestures for me to stand back. She smoothes the sheet on top of the table, points to my naked body and then jabs her index finger on top of the sheet. Oh! I'm supposed to remain on top of the sheet. Silly me. I lumber onto the table.

The massage begins and the small woman kneads, prods and pokes. She hammers my head. Pulls my toes. Cracks my back. My calves hover a half inch above the massage table. My hands squeeze into fists. This woman must be an interrogator for the People's Army for I'm ready to make up lies to get her to stop. And I do want her to stop but three things prevent me.

One, there's a language problem. She speaks no English. I speak no Mandarin.

Two, I'm proud. She can't really be hurting me; she's a dancer in a jewelry box and I'm Bigfoot.

Three, well, there was a third reason but I can't recall what it was because the tiny woman is now twisting my head like taffy.

I leave the massage room and crawl back to my cabin feeling as if I've just endured some kind of hazing ritual. I had expected the kind of massage I'm used to. The kind with dim lights, New Age music, and massage therapists who want to know where it hurts. The kind of massage where I'm allowed to crawl under the sheet and keep my private parts private.

As I unlock the door to my cabin, the appalling truth of the last sixty minutes hits me: I've become one of those not-so-rare Western travelers who is so used to having things a certain way that any deviation is considered inferior, abnormal, and just plain wrong. Foreigners have a phrase for people like us: Ugly Americans.

I slump onto the twin bed and gaze out the window at the slow brown river and misty green hillsides. How did this happen? More importantly, how did this happen to me? I mean, I've spent weeks and months at a time living in other countries, learning new customs, and trying to figure out how to say and buy everything from lightbulbs to hemorrhoid medication. I've negotiated with tow-truck drivers in Italy, confronted the threat of highway bandits in Guatemala, and shared cramped sleeping quarters on Spanish trains with fishermen from the Algarve Coast. To pass the time, my friend and I taught the fishermen how to play "Fish," the card game. Only we called it "Pescados."

What I'm saying is that I've always considered myself to be the antithesis of the ugly American traveler. I'm not loud, bossy, or insensitive. I'm not like Howard Stern or Texans with too much money or the New Yorker I once overhead in Portugal who squealed, "Look, honey! They even have sheet metal!" I don't expect sameness when I travel. I don't expect anything at all.

Yeah, right.

As I stare at the water drops on the window that frames the Yangtze River, I realize the tiny masseuse with the lethal fingers has taught me a lesson: I'm full of it. I have expectations in other countries just like everyone else does. In fact, I've probably had more expectations in China—and had more of them unmet—than anywhere I've ever been.

• • •

My struggle with unmet expectations started the second I landed in Beijing. After traveling twenty-four hours from Denver to Los Angeles to Tokyo and on to China, I was eager to see the "real" China. I wanted my first images to be those of rolling bicycles, muddy water buffaloes and thin people squatting with wooden bowls of rice. I yearned for dusty crowds and red lanterns and dirt floors.

Instead, I walked off the plane into a stark chrome and glass airport. I stepped onto a silent people mover and glided past billboards for dot com companies. I met our Chinese tour guide, "Leslie," who was wearing a black polo shirt emblazoned with a red Lucent Technologies logo. I checked my ticket stub. This couldn't be China. It looked more like Chicago. The undeveloped China in my mind didn't jive with the modern city I had landed in. There went expectation number one.

The next morning, during a tour of a Tiananmen Square, Leslie patiently explained to our small group of fourteen Americans that despite what we may have heard, hundreds of students were not killed during the 1989 military assault. "You heard wrong," he said. "A few people were killed but they were, how you say, hooligans. Hooligans from the countryside."

We rolled our eyes and looked at each other with virulent, self-righteous skepticism. *Oh puleeeeze.* Maybe we didn't get the whole story on Tiananmen Square, but we know, with the certainty of Westerners used to a free press, that hundreds of students were, in fact, killed. But this was China and we had expected a steady diet of lies and half-truths. After all, tour guides are state employees.

But two weeks into the trip, far away from Beijing, Leslie confided in us after dinner one night. As we sipped our tea, he explained that Tiananmen Square was crawling with plain-clothes officers of the People's Army who make sure the tour guides follow carefully written scripts in order to correct the misimpressions of foreigners. "I love my country," Leslie said. "But I hate my government." We were stunned. Sure, we had expected lies. But we were completely unprepared for such truth, trust, and emotion. There went expectation number two.

Expectation number three crumbled more gradually. Going to China, I had expected to sit back and take on the role of careful observer. I planned to click photos of smiling young girls, thin elderly men, and tired women picking tea leaves on steep hillsides. I had intended to record China like a young anthropologist jotting insightful comments in a worn leather notebook.

But while I had expected the Chinese people to be sources of fascination for me, I didn't expect to be a source of fascination for them. In countless cities I was grabbed by Chinese tourists eager to photograph my round eyes, tall frame, and light brown hair. I was the one who stood out from the crowd. Not them. As a middle-class white American girl who's used to blending in with the majority, it didn't occur to me that I would be the one worthy of inspection. Which just goes to show that no matter how well-traveled a person is, there's always room for new lessons to be learned.

Like that massage I told you about. Months later, I recounted the story of my Chinese massage to my own massage therapist, including all the hideous details about nudity in broad daylight.

"But Shari," she said to me. "Don't you know that Chinese massages are given with the clothes on?"

"On?" I asked.

"Yes," she replied. "The Chinese are modest. They don't disrobe."

I thought of the tiny massage therapist with the perfect black bangs.

"On?" I asked again.

" 'Fraid so."

Apparently, I wasn't the only one who got more than she bargained for.

Not Just Another Fish Story

I live next door to an eighty-three-year-old woman named Elmyna who was born in Mississippi, has cottony white, apple-doll hair, and is so short her legs dangle when she sits on the couch. I love Elmyna like a mother, which is to say that sometimes I want nothing more than to sit cross-legged at her feet and listen to iced-tea-on-the-veranda stories about her Southern childhood, whereas other times, I'd just as soon stab a fork in my neck.

See, Elmyna has this subtle way of making me feel guilty and imperfect, like a crippled child born to an Olympic medalist. Thanks to her observations, I'm now well aware that I don't brush my cat enough, that I should return calls more promptly, and that it is really much nicer to eat dinner from a plate that has been gently warmed in the oven, a fact she shared with me last Thanksgiving after I'd handed her a cold plate from the cupboard. I don't think Elmyna's mean-spirited; I think she believes I show potential for improvement.

Regardless of her intentions, I've come to be a bit anxious around Elmyna. Thus, it was with some trepidation that I agreed to watch her pet fish while she and her husband were in Arizona for two weeks. On the morning she left, I picked up the fish, a brilliant blue betta named Azure, along with a hand-written note that explained how her "poor spoiled baby" needed to be hand-fed a couple flakes of food several times a day.

Things between Azure and me got off to a good start. He'd

19

wriggle to the surface, eat the flakes I fed him, and then contentedly drift to the bottom of his bowl where he sat until the next mealtime. But about a week into our time together, I noticed Azure was not eating like he had been. Flakes of fish food swelled and bobbed on the water's surface. He stopped rising to greet me. And I began to feel the merest hint of alarm.

Looking to prevent Azure from catching a water taxi to the great beyond, I took to tapping on the glass to startle him. I cleaned his tank. I fed him more frequently, then starved him for a couple of days. Still, Azure remained on the bottom of the tank; the slow, tender flap of his gills the only indication he was still alive.

Elmyna returned home and I called to schedule a time to return her baby, who, by then, seemed a qualified candidate for home hospice. The phone was busy. I walked with the bowl next door. Nobody answered. I brought the bowl back home, and because I had plans that evening, set Azure on the counter and begged him to hang on for another day.

The next morning, Azure continued to hug the bottom of the tank and I decided if I was going to return a half-dead fish, at least the bowl should be clean. I removed Azure, emptied the water, scrubbed the bowl, refilled it with tap water, squeezed in a few drops of purifier, slid Azure back in, and called Elmyna again. Still no answer.

Two hours later, I noticed Azure listing to the left. I shook the bowl and he darted, gasping and desperate, to the top where he released a huge bubble and floated back to the bottom. Thinking the tap water must have been bad, I retrieved some bottled water from the garage, heated it to room temperature in the microwave, removed Azure, replaced the water, replaced Azure, and then watched as he floated in a slow zigzag back to the bottom. I called Elmyna again. Still no answer.

Three hours later, Azure was dead.

Panic set in and I did what any good friend who had done all she could to save a beloved family pet would do: I drove the pet store to try and trick her with a replacement.

Now, PetSmart normally has a shelf stacked with dozens of bettas in small plastic cups. But on the night of my emergency, there were just three left. Only one was blue and it had a fiery red stripe on its tail. I bought it.

When Elmyna saw the fish that night, her only comment was: "Azure, you're all red. What's she been feeding you?"

Although I should have been relieved to have gotten away with the switch, I obsessed about it. I avoided Elmyna during my walks around the neighborhood. I didn't answer the phone if I thought it might be her. In hindsight, telling her the truth would have been less stressful. But at the time, I was certain she'd turn the event into another opportunity to remind me how much I've yet to learn. Somehow, death and deception seemed preferable.

Elmyna and I finally talked by phone a week later and in the middle of a lovely conversation about her husband's constipation, she said to me: "Shari, that's not Azure is it?"

Stunned, all I could manage was: "Uh, no, uh, it isn't."

"Honey," she said, "I'm far too old and have grieved over too many things in life to worry about losing a silly old fish. I'm just sorry you felt you had to replace him. Now, when are we going to get you over here for dinner?"

And that was that. No lecture. No criticism. No well-meaning advice about the proper way to care for a fish. I think Elmyna must have sensed I was already so twisted with guilt and embarrassment that she didn't want to add to it. She let me off the hook with grace, respect, and her trademark Southern charm.

Despite my resistance to the lessons Elmyna has been trying to teach me, she found a way to tutor me in the art of understanding and forgiveness, which are far more important than a warm dinner plate and much more difficult to achieve.

Maybe I can learn a few things from her, after all. Like not being so defiant when someone offers advice, or protecting my ego when something goes wrong.

Next time, I'll tell Elmyna right off that her fish died while on my watch, and accept whatever comments I deserve. Not that there will be a next time, but, well, you know what I mean.

OPERA FOR DUMMIES

It started back in 1978 when I saw *Magic*, the Hollywood thriller starring Anthony Hopkins as a ventriloquist whose wooden dummy, "Fats," slowly goes crazy and embarks on a murderous rampage. The movie itself was terrifying. But it was the incessant airing of the TV commercial that really disturbed me. "Abracadabra, I sit on his knee," chanted the wide-eyed, high-voiced dummy while staring into the camera. "Presto-chango now he is me. Hocus pocus we take her to bed. Magic is fun. We're...dead."

Okay, maybe it doesn't sound so spine chilling in print. But at the time, the movie and its ad were menacing enough to instill a life-long fear of ventriloquists' dummies, marionettes, and other small, hand-painted facsimiles of human beings.

I imagine myself rising from a warm bed at two a.m. to let the dog out only to encounter a Charlie McCarthy-type character seated serenely at my kitchen table in the moonlight. "I'm glad you're awake," he'd say, his stiff lower jaw clacking shut as his eyes dart, Kewpie-like, toward the gleaming butcher knife gripped in his white-gloved dummy hand.

For years, I've been able to get through most days without obsessing about the sinister potential of puppets. But recently I was in Prague, in the Czech Republic, where marionettes are part of a—quote unquote—long and rich tradition.

On my first day there, walking through the narrow, cobblestone streets, I passed several shops selling the stringed puppets. Row upon row of expressionless marionettes hung limply from the walls, their hands and feet suspended in mid-air. There were rabbis and chefs and kings and witches, all of them silently beseeching passersby to give them life. I shuddered.

Angela looked at me. "They creep you out too, huh?" she asked.

I nodded as I scurried past the shops.

That night at dinner, Angela and I discussed our jointly held fear of marionettes and other inanimate human beings. Sipping our wine, we talked as if we were discussing something semi-rational, like politics. "The problem I have with them is their inability to reason," Angela explained.

Yes, I agreed. That was one of their deficiencies.

"I mean, when they are attached to human beings, they're fine," she continued. "It's when they're left to their own devices that I have trouble with them." Angela, too, had seen the ads for *Magic*.

After dinner, we walked through Prague's old town and noticed, in the corners of lighted store windows, colorful posters advertising a production of *Don Giovanni* by the National Marionette Theatre. Instead of sleek ads for cigarettes or posters promoting the latest Hollywood action film like you'd see in other European cities, Prague was all about puppets.

"No way," I proclaimed.

Angela agreed, thus securing her position as my favorite traveling companion.

• • •

The next day we were led on a walking tour of the city by a Czech woman who alternated her talk between English, for us, and French, for the other couple on the tour. We'd stop in front of a Gothic cathedral and she'd spend twenty minutes talking excitedly with the French couple about, I assumed, the history of the church. Her hands would make wide swooping circles overhead, as if she were describing the general craziness of church leaders during the Middle Ages. The French couple would nod their heads in rapid agreement. "Oui, oui, oui," they'd say, as if they were glad to have *finally* found someone who shared their passion for religious history.

When it was time for the English version, the guide would turn to us and say something along the lines of: "This is the Teyn Church. Its tower dominates the old town. Let's move on."

At one point, as I waited for the guide to finish a lengthy French narrative of the Charles Bridge, I spotted yet another marionette shop. This, in and of itself, was not unusual. What made this particular shop stand out was that its exterior speakers were broadcasting Michael Jackson's *Billie Jean* at levels loud enough to cause the last remaining Communists in that city to pack their identical, government-issue suitcases and flee up the Vltava River. On the street in front of the shop, a small Pinocchio marionette in yellow pants was break-dancing, its red feet clomping on the cobblestones at the behest of the college-age salesperson controlling its strings.

"Look," I exclaimed, before I knew what I was saying. "How cute!"

Angela stared at me as if I'd broken some unspoken covenant of the anti-marionette society. Then her eyes traveled to the break-dancing puppet. "They *are* less threatening when they dance," she conceded, if a bit reluctantly.

With the edge taken off, we soon found ourselves admiring the range and artistry of marionettes available for sale. We discussed how marionettes could still be popular in a city that has survived the Habsburgs and Communists, and now boasts sushi bars and Internet cafes. There must be something to this marionette business, we reasoned.

Our defenses crumbling, we scrambled for ways to keep our disdain of dummies intact. "The marionettes must just be for *tourists*," we scoffed, as if we weren't short-term visitors ourselves. When that didn't work, we tried snobbery, ranking marionette theater on the same cultural stratum as a monster truck rally.

But the more we questioned the allure of the puppets, the more we became fascinated by them. Over a beer and goulash that afternoon in a low-ceilinged Czech restaurant, Angela turned to me. "You know, I think we should see a marionette show, just to see what the fuss is about." I agreed, feeling strangely excited in a birthday-party kind of way.

Back at the hotel we asked the desk clerk to make reservations for the following night. While she cradled the phone and waited for the theater to answer, I sought confirmation for our decision. "Is it a *good* show?" I asked, eyebrows raised like a toddler seeking praise for a good deed.

The desk clerk sighed. She'd obviously heard this question a few thousand-million-jillion times. "Yes," she said, the word ending in a slight "zee" sound. "It's nice, if you like the *Don Giovanni* music." Somehow, I wasn't reassured.

• • •

We arrived at the theater early the next night. Although advertised as a "beautiful hall decorated in Art Deco style," what we encountered was a sad, dimly lit space with limp, red velvet curtains and plaster walls the color of split pea soup. The walls had been gouged in several places, leaving white, dusty scabs. In the lobby, a pale young woman stood beneath of clothesline of cheap plastic marionettes, hoping for a sale.

When it was time for the performance to start, instead of subtly dimming the lights or ringing a low chime as they do for performances in New York, the National Marionette Theatre of Prague sounded something akin to a school bell. Its insistent metal clapper reverberated painfully throughout the lobby. Startled, I didn't know whether to head to my seat, dart out the door for recess, or alert the captain that the submarine was taking on water.

The show began, and the first marionette to appear was Mozart, who was dressed in pink satin with white ruffles at the neck and sleeves. He had curly silver hair that looked slept on, and his round wooden face bore a slight resemblance to

Barbara Bush. As he jerkily "conducted" the imaginary orchestra—the real music was on tape—the other puppets made their appearances on the small stage. Controlled only by strings, they moved haltingly, as if walking across a rope bridge in high winds. It was going to be a loooong night.

As the production got underway, my snootiness kicked in. The backdrops were painted in a style that could best be described as Scenery 101. I could see the thick hands and cleavage of several of the puppeteers. How unprofessional was that? I felt like I was watching a fifth-grade talent show where at any moment a little Indian girl would be tied to the stake while her parents clapped their enthusiastic approval. Most unsettling of all was that the marionettes' faces didn't move. At all. Don Giovanni maintained the same painted-on, non-committal expression regardless of whether he was seducing the peasant girl Merlina or being engulfed by flames for his evil misdeeds.

And yet, despite myself, within a few short minutes I was smiling, a silly what's-the-harm-in-this grin that lasted the entire performance. I don't know if the grin appeared when I realized that puppeteers are supposed to be part of the act. Or when I realized this particular production of *Don Giovanni* was intended to be a comedy. Or when the Mozart marionette drank too much wine and fell asleep, loudly knocking his little wooden head on the edge of the imaginary orchestra pit.

Regardless, it dawned on me that the point of marionette theater is not to convince audience members that the puppets are real in an animated, Hollywood kind of way. The point was to give people an enjoyable, low-tech excuse for listening to great opera.

When the performance was over and the puppeteers emerged for their applause, it was clear from their pink cheeks and broad smiles that they took immense pride in their art. I stood and clapped like a stage parent.

• • •

As we walked back to the hotel after the show, Angela said,

"I'm glad we're not like those people who don't try new things because of fear or because they think something is beneath them."

"Me too," I said, gazing at the gold reflection of the city's lights in the river.

"Sometimes, it just takes learning about something to appreciate it," she reasoned, sounding a bit like the host of a children's television show.

I concurred, thinking of all the times in my life I've passed up opportunities because of fear, snobbery, or pre-conceived notions. I thought about how often I've let closed-minded assumptions color my enjoyment of an event. I thought about how foolish many of my long-held— and unexamined—fears and judgments really are. Maybe *Magic* had been so scary because I was eighteen when I saw it and, frankly, a lot of my life was tinged with terror at that point. I was on the verge of adulthood, after all, a status I had no idea how to manage. And still don't.

As we neared the hotel, Angela made one final comment about the show. "You know, those puppets didn't scare me At All."

"Me neither," I said, secretly wondering if I'd have time at the airport to purchase a souvenir marionette.

BOOK KEEPING

Michael Gulliford used to own my copy of *Rabbit, Run*. At least I think he did, for a faded $16.73 Visa receipt bearing his name was found on page eighty-six, which, if you've read the book, is the point at which Rabbit first encounters the minister, Jack Eccles.

I don't believe Michael Gulliford was the original owner of my yellowing, sixty cent paperback copy of the John Updike classic. The book was published in 1960; the receipt is dated 1986. Also, there's another name scrawled in slanted blue ink on the book's first page. It reads Carol Monsor or Carl Monsay. I'm not sure which.

But frankly, Carol/Carl doesn't interest me as much as Michael does. His receipt, missing the merchant's name, stirs my curiosity. Did a mall-averse Michael bring books along while shopping with his wife? Maybe he started the book over a solitary expense-account lunch in a midwestern Marriott. Perhaps Michael shoved the receipt inside the book while clearing his dresser in preparation for a date with a tall, wealthy brunette.

I thought about Michael every time I picked up my copy of *Rabbit, Run* and removed his receipt, which I used as a bookmark. I last inserted the receipt on page one hundred twenty-seven, the exact mid-point of the book. Classic or not, I couldn't bear to read any more about the preening and self-absorbed Harry Angstrom. As I removed the book from my nightstand, I wondered whether Michael liked the Rabbit any better than I had.

• • •

I bought *Rabbit, Run* at a used book sale held Mother's Day at the Denver Botanic Gardens. I hadn't planned to attend the book sale; I'd planned to spend a pleasant afternoon strolling the gardens with my mother and father, who happened to be in town that weekend.

Our walk among the blossomy trees began nicely enough, with Mom making the kind of polite, disaffected comments she's known for.

"Look at the pretty yellow flowers," she exclaimed. "And that's a BIG bush, isn't it?" Traveling with my mother is like being trapped inside a child's Dick-and-Jane story where only the obvious is worth mentioning.

"Yes Mom," I agreed. "That IS a big bush." She smiled and walked joyfully onward.

My father, however, was a different matter. Try though he might, Dad could not mask his disgust at having to walk among poppies and peonies on a warm, cloudless afternoon. Ten minutes into our family outing, he sat on a concrete bench next to an empty brown flowerbed, crossed his cardiganed arms over his chest, and refused to budge. By the time Mom and I finished touring the gardens, Dad had been pouting in the same rigid position for well over an hour.

His insolence so incensed me that I had no choice but to drag him to the used-book sale, something my father regards as the recreational equivalent of replumbing the house. How dare he be such a brat on Mother's Day? He wanted to pout? I'd give him something to pout about. With Dad stiffly situated on yet another bench, my mother and I walked into the sale.

The cost of books that day was three dollars a bag. Hardbacks, softcovers, biographies, novels, anthologies: hundreds of books in every category were stacked on the floor, lined along the tops of collapsible conference tables, and heaped into boxes that lined the perimeter of the cinder-block room. I eyed the banquet of books before me feeling like a refugee who'd just discovered Costco.

I picked up one of the plastic grocery bags piled near the entrance and set to work. My first stop was the fiction table where I immediately spotted Michael Gulliford's copy of *Rabbit, Run* as well as hardback editions of Philip Roth's *Goodbye Columbus,* and *Alias Grace* by Margaret Atwood. I plucked the books from the stack and dropped them into my bag.

Across the table, I spotted an older woman kick-pushing a half-filled cardboard box along the floor in front of her. Her squinty gray eyes were darting back and forth along the table. When her eyes came to rest on something near the middle of the table, I followed her line of sight and spotted a near-new copy of *Father Melancholy's Daughter* by Gail Godwin. Gail Godwin! I had to have that book, not only because I love Gail Godwin, but also because the title nicely summarized the experience I was having with my own father that day.

I slid my arm between two other shoppers and grabbed the Godwin book before the box lady could get it. I wasn't convinced she wanted it, but you can't take chances with that sort of thing. Used-book buyers can be so competitive.

I dropped *Father Melancholy's Daughter* into my bag and continued my slow circle around the fiction table. There were the usual suspects, including several Grishams, more Danielle Steeles than should be allowed to congregate in one location, and a tattered collection of science-fiction adventures.

As I neared the end of the table, I spotted two more finds that had been miscategorized: Truman Capote's *Music for Chameleons,* and Tom Wolfe's *The Right Stuff.* Yet as I reached to grab them, I recalled a promise I'd made to myself to think twice before hauling any more books into my house. At three dollars a bag, you'd think a little extravagance wouldn't have hurt anything. But after years of heedless bookstore gluttony, I've learned to restrain myself. Nowadays, I'm more likely to boast about the value of the books I returned to the shelves than I am to brag about what's in my bag. "I went to the

Tattered Cover the other day," I tell friends. "And I *didn't* spend eighty dollars."

Still, I was tempted. As pioneers in literary journalism, Capote and Wolfe didn't merely report on events in the world; their words invited readers to experience those events for themselves. And isn't that why I read? To live lives I wouldn't be able to otherwise? But I'd already chosen four novels. Did I really need two more?

• • •

For a long time I never stopped to question my acquisitive nature. But over the last few years, my collection of unread books has gotten so out of hand whenever I pass one of them in my house I feel a small magnetic tug of guilt. "Soon," I whisper, as I hurry by. "I'll get to you soon."

Six months ago, I bought a special bookcase to house all the books I've collected and yet to read. The bookshelf now holds more than ninety-five books, including used-book bargains, full-price impulse buys and my still-growing collection of leather-bound, gold-embossed Twentieth Century Classics published by Easton Press. Printed on specially milled, archival quality paper are the words of such authors as Henry James, Sylvia Plath, and Edith Wharton.

I started the collection two years ago, justifying the $49.50 per month, per book charge by claiming I needed to be steeped in the words of these authors so that I no longer had to fake understanding when well-read friends made references to literary heroes such as Dean Moriarity, Atticus Finch and, yes, Harry Angstrom. It's not that I've never read any modern classics. I just have a bad memory for them. My collection has, to date, cost more than $1200 and thus far I've only read Easton's edition of *On the Road* by Jack Kerouac, which goes to show how expensive this obsession can be.

Why not borrow books from friends? Because that, too, is fraught with complications. For instance, I have this friend—let's call her Generous Jen—who routinely comes to dinner bearing an armload of books she just knows I will love. And I probably will. Jen and I have similar tastes and if she likes a book, chances are excellent I will too. But the loan of her books comes with such a burden.

The problem is two-fold. First, since the books are a loan, I feel compelled to read and return them promptly. But what if I don't want to read them right away, or at all? Is that insulting, like telling someone her child is fat?

The second challenge is that even though Generous Jen can give books to friends with the cheerful abandon of a person handing out flyers at the mall, I can't. In fact, it horrifies me to think how easily people give away books they've read. I mean, authors spend years putting words to the page and getting them published. It just doesn't seem right for someone to read a book and then hand it to a friend with the comment: "I'm done with it. It's yours now."

Actually, my biggest fear is that if I accept a book from Jen she'll expect me to offer a few in return. Which would be fine, if she'd give them back. But you can't trust generous people. They take your books, read them, and then pass them along to someone else. Before you know it, your book has passed through more hands than a beach ball bouncing through the crowd at a baseball game.

Since borrowing is out of the question, maybe it does make sense to buy the Capote and Wolfe books. But with dozens of unread books already on my shelves, the question arises again: *Do I need them?*

• • •

Marketing consultants will tell you that people don't acquire things like books because they need them, all justifications to the contrary. People need things like fruit and toothbrushes and gasoline. But books are typically bought with what is laughingly called "disposable income." As if, given a choice, we could either toss our leftover money down a storm drain, or buy a book.

According to the researchers, people choose to spend their disposable income based a complex set of emotional drivers. They buy because they're afraid, greedy, depressed or trying to fill voids in their lives. I'd like to think I buy books for more substantial reasons, like love. Yet I admit books have spackled some holes in my life.

As the lone brown-eyed brunette among a trio of blonde, blue-eyed sisters, I frequently felt like a foreigner at the dinner table. But it wasn't just the physical disparities that separated us. There were also vast differences in temperament.

My sisters spent their free time shopping at the mall with fashionable friends who knew the difference a well-placed accessory could make. Me, I preferred shoplifting, like the time in eigth grade I went to J.C. Penney with Audrey Harding and, on a dare, walked out wearing a new yellow bra with the tags still on over the bra I already had on. That night, sitting in bed wearing my new yellow bra under my nightgown, I recall reading *I Never Promised You a Rose Garden* and being relieved to discover I wasn't the only teenager searching for the planet where she really belonged.

As a shy kid, books allowed me to try on other, more comfortable identities without the torment of actually having to talk to someone.

For instance, I read *Joy in the Morning* and tried, unsuccessfully, to envision myself as a young newlywed making coffee and eggs for my husband before he left for work.

I read *Go Ask Alice* and spent a week picking my cuticles and mumbling like a teenager in drug rehab.

I read the Nancy Drew mysteries and felt a shimmer of recognition when I learned about Nancy's brown-haired tomboy girlfriend, George Payne.

As a kid, the places, people and events I read about in books were so real that I frequently chose reading about life to actually participating in it. I once went to summer camp, for example, and spent the majority of time in my tent reading a book about a girl at summer camp.

It took years and thousands of pages, but books eventually taught me what kind of person I am, which is a Joan Didion-John Irving-Susan Orlean kind of person. Better yet, books allowed me to join the community of readers who feel as passionate about the written word as I do—which is probably why I care so much about Michael Gulliford and his impression of Rabbit Angstrom.

But now that I am my own person and I have my own community, do I still need books the way I used to? Did I need to add Truman Capote and Tom Wolfe to my collection to reinforce my place in the world?

• • •

I looked at my father sitting outside the book sale next to an enormous fan-shaped palm and began to feel guilty. What was I doing scooping up more books to add to my already jammed bookcase? I could read a book a week and not have a legitimate need for a new one for almost two years. Just as I was ready to set down my plastic bag, my mother walked up to me.

"Look! Look at what I've found!" she said, presenting me with a small stack of true-crime paperbacks. "I love these stories!" She set the books into my sack, and turned away. "This is fun!" she called over her shoulder. "I'm going to find more goodies!"

Goodies.

That's exactly what books are. Goodies that connect me to other places. Goodies that teach me about other lives. Goodies that keep me company and enliven my mind and ease the torment of waiting for a delayed flight. Did I need any more justification than that to buy a book? I watched my mother smiling over a table of used travel books and made my decision.

I walked back to the table and without another thought dropped Truman Capote's *Music for Chameleons* into my bag, followed by *The Right Stuff*, Tom Wolfe's tale of astronaut courage. I then proceeded to spend the next fifteen minutes filling two plastic bags to the bursting point.

My haul? Twenty-nine books, which included twelve hardbacks, nine novels, a collection of essays by Joyce Carol Oates, quotes about writing by Ernest Hemingway, Arthur Miller's *Death of a Salesman*, and several reference books, including one called *Books That Made a Difference*. The bags also included my mother's three true-crime novels, and Michael Gulliford's copy of *Rabbit, Run*. The total bill? Six bucks. But I could have easily spent twelve.

I took the books home, laid them on the kitchen table in neat little rows, and beheld them like a duck hunter viewing a collection of cooling carcasses in the back of a pickup truck. The marketing experts are right. I do need these things. And although Michael Gulliford was able to part with *Rabbit, Run*, I don't expect I'll be able to do the same.

TALKIN' ABOUT CHICKEN

Yesterday, I'd just gotten comfortable at my favorite table in my neighborhood Starbucks when I noticed two seventy-somethings seated at the table next to me. Although they sat mere inches from one another, they communicated as if they were standing on opposite ends of a dark mountain tunnel.

"I'M WILLING TO GO FAR FOR GOOD CHICKEN," bellowed the gentleman in yellow pants on the left.

"YOU DO LOVE YOUR CHICKEN," agreed his companion, a man whose enormous black glasses made him look like a political cartoon.

I smiled at the poultry lover in a subtle I-like-chicken-too kind of way. Then I removed a fresh yellow highlighter from my pocket, took a sip of my latte, and began to read through the folder of interview notes I'd brought with me. I read one sentence before my concentration was interrupted.

"KNOW WHO HAS SURPRISINGLY GOOD CHICKEN?" queried the man with the glasses.

"WHO?" asked Yellow Pants eagerly.

"Red Lobster."

"Red *Lobster?*"

"SWEAR TO GOD."

Yellow Pants couldn't accept this information. He did, however, agree the shrimp platter was second to none. Yellow Pants then went on to explain, in stupefying detail, the exact location of every good chicken restaurant within ninety miles of the Denver metropolitan area.

I put down my highlighter and began drumming my fingers on the table wondering how long the chicken chatter would continue. I looked around and noticed two men in dark suits sitting at a table on my right. They were tapping into their Palm Pilots, jotting notes onto a legal pad, and strategizing about an upcoming sales meeting. They were doing exactly what people are *supposed* to be doing at Starbucks: working.

As I listened to the older gentlemen on my left and the salesmen on my right it dawned on me that the biggest difference between retirement and the working years is the ability—and desire—to talk about chicken. At length. I wish I had time to think about chicken, I mutter to myself as I jam my folder into my briefcase and head off in search of a quieter table. But I'm busy. I have deadlines. I have to multitask whenever possible.

Even my idle time is filled with projects and purpose.

Take running, for example. When I go for a run, instead of admiring the daffodils that are starting to push through the hard-packed winter dirt, I try to generate new story ideas and make sure I keep my heart rate at seventy percent of maximum for at least twenty-five minutes.

When I go to the dentist, instead of wasting time in the waiting room by reading about the latest celebrity breakup, I compare the allocation of my stock portfolio against the allocations suggested in *Money* magazine. No sense wasting a good twenty minutes.

I'm not like this person I know who just converted to part-time and now leaves work at one o'clock everyday to work on his golf game. If I took off at one o'clock, I'd expect myself to write a novel. Or learn Japanese. By dinner.

• • •

I didn't realize how bad this constant do-think-plan mentality was until last night when I found myself alone in a restaurant waiting for a friend. I didn't have a notebook so I couldn't jot notes or plan the next day's activities. I didn't have a cell phone so I couldn't check voice mail or leave impressive after-hours messages for my editors. I hadn't even brought a report or magazine to read.

So, I read the menu. Four times. I looked out the window. I read the menu again. I asked for a glass of water. I read the menu again. I checked my watch. I started to sweat and within the space of minutes, I'd wrapped my arms around my waist and begun to take deep sucking breaths like a drug addict curled in a darkened corner of an abandoned warehouse.

By the time my friend arrived fifteen minutes later I was utterly disconsolate. Not because she was late but because I'd been forced to spend fifteen minutes—nine hundred whole seconds—idle and alone with my thoughts. There were things I could have been doing, should have been doing. But I went to the restaurant unprepared. The time had been wasted.

After I explained my dismay to my friend—who was not nearly as apologetic for her tardiness as I thought she should have been—she looked at me and asked, gently, "Why did you think you had to do anything? Quiet time is good thing, you know."

And then it dawned on me. The ability to cogitate on things like chicken and Red Lobster are not a side effect of one's employment status; they are a function of one's perspective. My friend was right: idle time is not wasted time. Taking time out, even for fifteen minutes, allows you to reflect on your life, generate new ideas and appreciate things like chicken and the many ways it can be cooked and how many other animals, when cooked, taste like chicken. It's why people take vacations and have Sundays off and why there are wonderful things in the world like books and plays and champagne and hiking trails. Idle time may not be good for our careers, but it's essential to our souls.

So here's my challenge: for the next week try to take time every day to be alone with your thoughts. Hide your to-do list. Turn off the radio in your car. Look at the clouds. Go to bed a half-hour earlier without a book. Do something because, well, just because. Then, when you've figured out how to be idle—how to do or think or talk about anything that pleases you even for a brief amount of time every day—let me know how it goes. I'll be with the two old guys at this great new chicken restaurant down the street.

WHINERS NEED NOT APPLY

Sometime last summer I decided to host a pity party and invite all my friends. Well, not all my friends, exactly. Only those whose livelihoods might have, like mine, been suffering from the downward slide of the economy. To make the guest list, invitees would have to possess the ability to grumble, gripe, groan, fuss, snarl, scream, fret, rant and complain—preferably all at the same time. I wanted world-class whiners at my party. Optimists need not apply.

The idea for the party came about following several back-to-back conversations with different editors, all of whom relayed to me different versions of the same scenario: advertising sales are down, there are fewer magazine pages to fill, so we don't have as many assignments for contract writers like you. Almost overnight, or so it seemed, the regular work I'd come to count on disappeared.

"Sorry," my editors said. "But *do* keep in touch."

But I didn't. And instead of bucking up and marketing myself to new clients, instead of choosing to view this "challenge" as an "opportunity" like I'd been taught in so many motivational seminars, I chose to complain. Loudly. With great chest-heaving drama. Picture Joan Crawford, wrist to forehead, lying in a bed strewn with movie magazines and you have some idea of my approach. Why tire myself getting new business, I argued, when sympathy was so much easier to elicit?

The beauty of my pity party was that it was not time or location dependent. Instead it was an ad hoc celebration that occurred on the phone and over dinner, and lasted from mid-

49

summer until well into October. The lengthy guest list included such luminaries as other freelance "worst-market-in-fifteen years" writers; graphic "clients-just-aren't-spending-money" designers; and software "we're-wondering-how-to-make-it-through-December" executives. These people made the cut because I knew they'd confirm my belief that the economy was in the toilet and there was no work to be found. Anyone whose work might be humming along as usual or, worse yet, improving—this includes criminal lawyers and unemployment counselors—were conveniently left off the invitation list.

Whenever I met a fellow partygoer I'd ask, perhaps a bit too eagerly: "So how bad is it? Any bill collectors yet? Tell me again about losing that contract and this time don't leave anything out."

It was such a bad case of selective perception that I interpreted everything around me as proof that work was not available. I'd spot smiling families playing in the park and assume the parents must've lost their jobs. I'd see people laughing at restaurants and assume they were drunk, probably as a way of masking their deep internal misery.

I was so convinced I'd never be hired for another writing assignment that I stopped even trying to find work. I didn't call any of my corporate clients. I didn't pitch new story ideas to editors. Instead, I stayed home, played computer solitaire, and wished I'd saved more money.

Then, I met with my personal coach, a wise and wonderful woman whom I pay to keep me on track in life.

"Shari," she said gently. "All of us create our own realities. Your situation seems hopeless because that's how you've decided it should be. How would you act if you knew the economy was good and work was available?"

"Ummm," I said. "I guess I'd line up some story *ideas?*" I answered her tentatively, as if asking a question.

"Good," she said. "Then what would you do?"

"Ummm, I guess I'd call some *editors?*"

Then, doing her best not to sound like my mother, she asked

me: "Have you called any editors lately?"

I got the picture.

I spent the following Sunday researching potential story ideas and preparing letters for my magazine clients. I sent the letters out via e-mail and within twenty-four jaw-dropping hours I had three new assignments. A week later, a fourth came in, and two weeks after that, an associate of mine called about some international speaking opportunities.

When I first started in business for myself, an experienced entrepreneur told me that even during down times I should always project a positive, successful image. So what if clients hadn't paid me in months or that I hadn't changed out of my terrycloth robe in days? Every inquiry about my business should be met with the same response: "It's terrific! Never been better!"

I subscribed to this fake-it-til-you-make-it philosophy for a long time and you know what? It works. But apparently, last summer, after years of round-the-clock, worry-free assignments, I had forgotten that success, confidence and happiness are often a matter of where you place your attention. When I finally got out of bed, picked up the movie magazines and began to act like a successful professional, the work appeared with stunning rapidity.

My pity party is now over, thankfully, and friends who grew tired of my bleak line of questioning are no longer darting down the baby aisle in supermarkets in order to avoid me. My professional confidence index is up and I'm now looking for optimists to celebrate with me. Whiners need not apply.

SEEK AND YE SHALL...SEEK

I've searched for God the way a pig roots for truffles. Sniffing under this altar. Chasing after that sermon. Certain if I stayed in the damp forest of agnostic confusion long enough that one day, trees would part, trumpets would sound, and the golden rays of faith would lead me toward eternal bliss.

Given my history, it comes as no surprise to find myself on this early November morning speeding down an empty freeway in bright sunshine toward a weekend seminar on Zen Buddhism. I'm speeding because I slept late, and because my friend Lezah and I failed to pre-register, and because a quick stop at a drive-through espresso hut resulted in several pissed minutes trying to mop coffee out of my jeans with a used Kleenex.

I pick Lezah up at her house and we jointly decide that if the line to the seminar is too long we can simply cut in to prove to the other budding Buddhists that we need the instruction more than they do.

"And if that doesn't work," Lezah says, stopping to take a pull from her latte, "we can spend the day shopping."

• • •

I was first introduced to religion at age four when my parents enrolled me in a private Presbyterian school. The religious underpinnings of the school weren't the main selling point; it was the fact the administration was willing to admit me into kindergarten even though I was just four years old. Classes

53

were held in a white, three-room bungalow next to a small stucco Presbyterian church. The minister was the principal; his wife, the teacher; their daughter, my best friend. For a suburb of San Francisco in the mid-1960s it was all very *Little House on the Prairie.*

An obvious if unspoken expectation for accepting me into the school was that my family would agree to become members of the church. My parents, who exhibited as much religious fervor as a toaster, respectfully dropped my sisters and I off every Sunday morning at 8:45 equipped with our rubber, squeeze-in-the-middle coin purses filled with two quarters each for the collection plate. About the only religious lessons learned during the two years I spent in that school were the story of Noah's ark and how to set my quarters into the wooden collection bowl so they didn't clatter in an obvious way.

Instead of expanding my knowledge about the Almighty, my early schooling supplied me with more questions than answers. Why didn't my parents go to church if it was so important? Was being a Presbyterian like being a Californian? And if God truly wanted the best for everybody why did he give me a younger sister? They were the questions of a five-year-old, but the pattern was set. Religion, for me, became about seeking, not finding

• • •

Lezah and I walk into the Zen temple and remove our shoes, as instructed. We head to the registration table and learn from a pleasant, plain-faced woman that although we are the first drop-ins to arrive she's not sure we'll be admitted. I head to the bathroom to scrub the coffee from my jeans, then rejoin Lezah in the lobby.

The building that houses the Denver Zen Center is different from what I'd envisioned. Having been to Buddhist temples in China, I'd been expecting a massive gold Buddha surrounded by shiny black woodwork. I'd envisioned worshippers outside bowing with smoky bouquets of red incense. Instead, the

Denver Zen Center is housed in an old stone building located in a treed residential neighborhood. The main level consists of a large, shell-shaped auditorium with fold-up wooden seats and high bright windows. Except for the faint smell of incense, it's a lot like the theater on my college campus.

Lezah and I sip our coffee and watch participants line up at the registration table. Five minutes pass and we check the roster to see if there's space to admit us. Five minutes later, we check again. The pleasant woman informs us she still doesn't know for sure if we'll be admitted. We ask her to write down our names believing if we aren't somehow recorded in a semi-official way our spots will be given to some pushy Buddhist who may come after us. Apart, Lezah and I are self-conscious and tentative. Together, we're Leona Helmsley on Tanqueray.

• • •

After my two-year stint at the Presbyterian school, I transferred to public school, stopped going to the Christian church, and started learning what it was like to be Catholic; or rather, what it was like to not be Catholic.

The blue-collar, middle-class suburb I grew up in was populated by first- and second-generation Italian, Hispanic and Filipino immigrants, the majority of whom honored the Virgin Mary, attended weekly catechism, and dutifully ate fish sticks every Friday. My family was different, not only because we sprang from the upper-middle class descendants of Northern Europeans, but also because we didn't adhere to any religious discipline.

I envied the saintly rituals of my friends. *I* wanted to earnestly discuss the importance of giving up Skittles for Lent. I wanted to know what it felt like to make up lies for the priest during confession. I wanted to walk into homeroom with a thumbprint smudge between my eyes on Ash Wednesday to demonstrate that I, too, had a direct-dial connection to God. But we weren't Catholics, my parents explained, while failing to elaborate on what, exactly, we might be instead. I felt so excluded from the Catholic commonwealth I was convinced I couldn't say "Bless You" when someone sneezed.

For a while I tried to fit in by wearing a gold cross to school. But the cross felt hot and fraudulent, like rosary beads on a stripper, and while it helped me to pass for Catholic at school, I'd take pains to remove it before I got home. Two blocks from my suburban tract house, I'd stop, set my books on the cool sidewalk, and when I was sure no neighbors were peering through their windows, I'd reach behind my neck, unclasp the chain and bury the cross deep in the pocket of my pea coat.

I didn't actually enter a Catholic church until my senior year of high school when friends invited me to Mass on Christmas Eve. Although they explained the liturgy ahead of time, I became completely unhinged as the religious Jazzercise of the Mass unfolded. The aerobic cycle of standing, sitting, standing, kneeling, standing, bowing, etcetera, made me relieved, for the first time, that my parents hadn't pushed religion down my proverbial throat. How did all that ritual get anyone closer to God? I just didn't get it.

• • •

After twenty minutes of waiting, Lezah and I are granted admission to the Buddhist seminar and we take our seats in the second row of the auditorium among thirty or so other participants. The room is silent except for the occasional echoey cough or shuffling of feet. A temple volunteer walks to the front of the room and introduces the Sensei, or teacher of the temple.

The Sensei, a white man who is barefoot and wearing a black, floor-length robe, walks slowly toward a raised platform covered by a flat black pillow. He sits down, crosses his legs into the lotus position, folds his robe underneath his legs, and clips a lapel microphone to his collar. This takes a good ten minutes, during which everyone in the audience is held in rapt attention. Although he is thin and shaven bald, the Sensei clearly has presence. It's not the fiery-cheeked presence of a Southern evangelist, or the commanding rigidity of a military officer. Instead, his is a tranquil, confident presence that pulls us forward in our seats. This tranquility is what we've plunked down fifty bucks to find.

The Sensei begins to deliver a methodical, if abbreviated, overview of Zen Buddhism. He tells us the story of Buddha who renounced his family and material wealth for a life of contemplation in the forest. He talks about how Buddha recognized that all of life is suffering and that so much of that suffering comes from inside. Anger, resentment, ego, desire, satisfaction, hate, judgment, indeed the whole hit parade of human emotion starts at the corner of First and Main in our minds. But if we can dial down the Almighty Self, the Sensei says, if we can eliminate the bloated self-concept that causes us to feel less than we should or better than we are, then we can eliminate the cause of our suffering. This, in turn, can't help but make us more accepting and less judgmental.

Lezah and I look at each other like a long-married couple who've just been won over by a travelling vacuum cleaner salesman. Yes, our silent nods seem to say. Our minds are filthy mats riddled with lint. Yes, we do want a better way to keep the dust down. We're just about to ask where to sign up when the Sensei starts speaking again, his voice stern. "I want to make one thing perfectly clear, and that is Buddhism is not like psychology," he says. "Psychology is about improving the self. Buddhism is about getting rid of the self. It's about getting rid of all the attachments you think you need to be yourself. Buddhism," he adds decisively, "is not about doing or having or growing or overcoming. It's about being." The Sensei falls silent and closes his eyes.

I watch the calm man in the black robe and think about what he's just said. While I agree with his basic premise, and I do desperately want to stop the squeaky hamster wheel of thought that rolls in my own mind, I'm a bit concerned. After all, I'm a writer who's part of a growing legion of essayists who narcissistically believe the only events worth writing about are those that involve themselves. If I succeed in releasing my self from myself, what will I write about?

Lezah shares a different concern during the break. "Does giving up my attachments mean I have to give up golf?" she asks.

After the break, we return to the auditorium and the Sensei directs us to introduce ourselves. Starting at the front left corner and zigzagging through the rows, each of the participants cites his or her name and occupation. Among us are web masters, architects, landscape designers, physical therapists and retirees. After the Sensei's talk about self—and what an artificial construct it is—I'm struck by how insignificant our career titles seem. Other people must feel the same way because they begin to state their positions tentatively, as if asking a question. "I'm Jill," says one young blonde woman, "and I'm a technical *writer?*"

After the introductions, the question-and-answer period begins and it's clear other people are struggling with the same issues I am. "If I give up my self," says one woman who makes little air quotes around the world 'self' with her fingers, "I'm afraid I'll be boring; that I won't feel any emotion." The Sensei assures her this won't be the case. Lezah asks about the difficulties of giving up material attachments in a culture that reinforces materialism at every turn. "I mean, I *like* my things," she says. The Sensei tells her that possessions, in and of themselves, aren't the issue. One man wants to know if he has to become a vegetarian. All of us, it seems, like the idea of getting rid of attachments, but we're skeptical about the practicality of it all.

The Sensei reassures us that we will still feel pain and happiness, that we won't lose our personalities or the ability to focus, and that we can still enjoy the things in our lives, but that the practice of Buddhism will make us more mindful of those things and more able to question the significance we place upon them. "If you choose to follow this path," he says, "you'll find you won't have to give up bad habits. They'll give up you."

• • •

After the self-conscious struggle to fit in with the Catholics, the stumbling, five-and-half-year drunk known as college came as a welcome relief.

I'd enrolled at California State University Chico in 1979, a year after *Playboy* magazine named it the Number One Party School in the nation. It was the kind of national honor that inspired selfless devotion, and students there worked to maintain the title the way some schools strive to produce future presidents. The closest I ever came to a spiritual discussion during that time occurred one night while sitting on the floor of my dorm room armed with a tall blue bong. I took a spectacular hit of dope, held it tight in my chest, and then exhaled with the kind of expertise that comes from rigorous daily practice.

"Do you ever wonder how we got here?" I asked my roommate Marla, a pragmatic Valley girl from Southern California.

"Yeah," she said. "You're from San Francisco. I'm from L.A. We're in Chico. How wild is that?"

"No, I don't mean here, as in this room," I said, pointing disgustedly at the carpet. "I mean here as in, you know, this world, this planet, these bodies." I waved the bong above me in wide smoky circles to underscore the vastness of my question.

Marla watched the smoke trails, obviously contemplating the deep black origins of our lives. I waited, hungrily, for her insight. Maybe she had a better grasp on the meaning of it all than I did.

"Wow," she said after something like half an hour. "I'm really high."

I'm now fairly certain my spiritual growth would have blossomed if it weren't for my glassy-eyed friends. Why I looked to roommates for answers to holy questions I'm not sure, especially since everyone I knew then had renounced the faiths they'd grown up with. Catholics, Jews, Methodists, Episcopalians— every last one of them seemed to be actively trying to cancel the lifetime memberships of their childhood religions. Having grown up outside of the church, I had nothing to reject, no religious conditioning to declare on my transition across the border to adulthood.

In spite of this, or perhaps because of it, my own search for understanding lingered. I don't know if I was searching for God or religion or a "higher power" as my AA friends called it. What I do know is that I was tired of feeling left out, and I envied people who, I assumed, understood some cardinal truth about human existence that I did not. Even friends who'd rejected religion continued to talk about "the big guy" or "the man upstairs." They may have scorned catechism but most of them managed to maintain a relationship with some larger, all-knowing something-or-other that helped them find peace of mind when they needed it.

In my mid-twenties, I searched for this all-knowing something-or-other in a variety of places. I backpacked through Europe, stood in cool musty cathedrals and willed myself, unsuccessfully, to feel its presence. I dove into the chalk-scented pages of Aristotle, Krishnamurti and Rilke, searching for the wisdom in their words. I joined feminist groups and attended weeklong festivals in Yosemite National Park with unshaven "womyn" who chanted in sweat lodges, deciphered their auras, and were careful to publicly announce whenever men would be present. "There will be Men On The Land tomorrow morning from eight to ten," announced a topless woman in a white apron. "They will be cleaning the toilets by the drug-and alcohol-free camping zone."

The pagan, Mother Earth, goddess-worshipping crowd re-ignited my interest in spirituality and for a time, in a desperate hunt for metaphysical wisdom, I invested heavily in Tarot cards, runes and astrological charts. I even saw a three hundred pound palm reader named Madame Ruby who wore sleeveless muumuus and doled out sage advice from an improbably dainty wicker chair. "On the outside, you seem confident," she said, her mottled arms quivering as thin wicker creaked below her. "But inside, you're much less certain." I bit my lower lip and nodded, struck speechless by her profound insight.

When all my metaphysical wandering led to the same dead end, when all the money spent in New Age boutiques left me just as hollow and wanting as ever, I entered psychotherapy. Maybe I could find answers and understanding from a couch. Months later, I was no closer to God but I had fallen in love with a woman—a move that put a decisive end to the God question, at least for a while. I grew thankful, to whomever or whatever might be responsible, that even though I still hadn't found a god or goddess that worked for me, at least I didn't have to bare the disappointed presence of a stern, finger-wagging God as did so many of my previously religious gay friends. Being newly out, there was enough to get used to without having to listen to the endless tut-tutting of the Almighty.

Over the next few years, I entered a long-term relationship with a woman, developed a writing career, bought a house, and got bored. Surely, there had to be something more than this, I lamented, blowing at my bangs like the weary housewife in a bath-oil commercial. I tried piano lessons. I learned to cook. I traveled. It was a nice life, I told myself, using the word "nice" the same way women use it to describe their sex lives to each other at college reunions. Nice, as in boring. Nice, as in routine.

Given the state of complacency I'd entered into, I was easy pickins when the local United Church of Christ announced their status as an "open and affirming" church. It was at a time when Colorado's fundamentalist Christians had declared open season on gays and lesbians and succeeded in passing a state ballot measure forbidding government agencies from extending civil rights protections to homosexuals. Wanting to distinguish itself from the Bible beaters behind the measure, the UCC sent out a wide, warm welcome to all the gays and lesbians in my northeast Denver neighborhood. Their message? "We're not one of *those* churches."

My piano teacher, who directed the church choir, told me of the church's intent and invited my partner and me to service

one Sunday. She beamed as she introduced us to the congrega-
tion, as if I were a first-year piano student who'd just mastered
Tschaikovsky's first concerto. She asked us to stand in our pew
and unbelievably, we did. Apparently, the intimidating power
of piano teachers does not diminish with age. My partner and
I stood there in our short haircuts, dark blue blazers and flat
loafers, the only thing missing was a sign over our heads that
said: "Lesbian Couple. Established circa 1985." The church
members applauded. Yes, *applauded*. After years spent feeling
on the outside either because I had no religion or because
I was gay, here I was being given an ovation for being both
homosexual and in a church.

After that first Sunday, my partner opted out of church but
I kept going. I liked the liberal sermons and the songs and the
way the other church members flocked to me over coffee and
cookies in the vestibule afterward. "How is your sig-ni-fi-cant
other," they would ask, emphasizing each syllable like children
practicing a new vocabulary word.

I confess: I liked the insider feeling I got at the church. The
people were warm and I felt welcome and a part of things—for
a time. But after about three months, my attendance at church
began to seem more beneficial for the other members than it
was for me. I was Exhibit A in their effort to prove their lov-
ing open-mindedness. But even this wasn't the real reason I
left. I left because I couldn't assemble the weekly collection of
psalms and proverbs and hymns into any coherent picture of
God and how he—or she—might fit into my life. Sitting in
that church didn't transform me anymore than the Presbyterian
service in kindergarten, or the Catholic Mass in high school,
or the New Age rituals of my twenties.

I left the church and my eight-year relationship ended. Even
though they weren't related, the intersection of these events
did propel me onto a more determined path to find spiritual
wisdom. But it was no longer because I wanted to know how
we got here or where we're going. It was because I needed something to give comfort when life and love disappointed me.

• • •

After the Sensei's talk, Lezah and I and the other seminar participants are led downstairs to a dimly lit space called the zendo, which is the Zen temple's meditation hall. As we shuffle inside, our eyes are drawn to the only structure in the room: a square cherrywood altar on top of which sits a small gold Buddha. Looking down, we notice flat black pillows on the floor. We sit on these, forming a horseshoe around the altar.

A stocky young white man sporting a shaved head and brown robe lights some incense, bows, and seats himself cross-legged at the base of the altar. His bulk hints at a former career as a college fullback. "Hi," he says. "My name is Joseph."

Joseph spends the next hour detailing the Zen method of zazen, or group meditation. He tells us how to enter and leave the zendo, when to bow, how to sit, what posture to take, and what we should do with our bodies throughout the meditation. "Your eyes should be open slightly," he says. "Let your gaze go soft three feet on the floor in front of you. Hold your head upright, chin tucked in slightly. Your shoulders? Relaxed and open. Arms? Hanging loosely at your sides. Okay, men? Ten-HUT!" Actually, Joseph doesn't really say ten-hut, but I fully expect him to, given the military precision of his instructions.

I strive to follow along. I adjust my head, my gaze, my shoulders, my back, my arms and my palms. Then I adjust my shoulders again. All of this reminds me of the countless times men in plaid have stopped me on golf courses and tried to correct my swing. "Keep your head down, young lady! Follow-through on that swing!" I start to get so confused by all the detail Joseph is throwing at us that golf is actually starting to sound like a relaxing alternative.

After we've chosen our favored positions on the plump round pillows known as zafus—I choose to straddle mine—Joseph instructs us on the proper method of breathing. "When you breathe in, say 'one' in your mind," he says. "When you exhale, say 'one' again. Count like this until you reach the number ten and then start over." The point, Joseph explains, is for us to keep bringing our minds back from the endless litany of thought to the simple acts of breathing and counting. The practice is designed to help us empty our minds and focus solely on sitting. "If your thoughts get away from you, simply start over at the count of one," Joseph says. "And trust me, they *will* get away from you."

As Joseph speaks, my emotions vacillate between two poles. At one extreme, I feel a sincere, childlike interest in learning how to meditate properly. At the other, I feel like I'm being subtly brainwashed and if I'm not careful I will soon be swathed in white cotton and handing out daisies at Denver International Airport. I'm finding it's not that easy to rid oneself of the mocking ways of an outsider.

Joseph ends his talk by explaining that after the break we will sit for two twenty-five minute sessions of *zazen*, interspersed by a five-minute walking meditation known as *kinhin*. The mission will be to keep our minds away from thought and focused solely on the here and now.

"Did you catch all that?" I ask Lezah on the break.

She shakes her head. "Not hardly. I think we should just follow the others."

This worries me because in a sense I've been following others all my life. At the womyn's festivals in Yosemite, I stripped off my shirt and bra in an effort to fit into the crowd of barebreasted, nature-loving women. As I recall, I drank a lot of beer that weekend because I discovered that clutching plastic cups of beer in each hand allowed me to keep my breasts strategically shielded. I *hated* walking topless in the woods, but it felt like something I should do. What might I have to do here, in the zendo, to get it and fit in? And why should I care? I'm here to find peace of mind, right, not join a sorority. Or am I? Maybe community is part of what I'm seeking.

Lezah and I finish our cups of tea and walk with the other students back to the zendo. As instructed, we bow to the statue of Buddha upon entering. We bow to each other across the room. We turn and bow before sitting on our pillows. Far from the picture of practiced unison, the thirty of us newcomers are popping up and down at wildly different intervals like a Buddhist version of the Whack-a-Mole arcade game. After several minutes of rustling confusion, we settle onto our pillows for group meditation.

I'd read a lot about meditation before coming to the Denver Zen Center. I'd learned it is the central point of Buddhist practice, the fulcrum upon which followers balance their lives. Adherents claim daily meditation helps free the mind of its entanglements, which allows people to gain clarity and a sense of connectedness with others. This, in turn, helps us become more compassionate, more accepting of change, and more able to withstand the struggles of daily life. All in all, it's a pretty good deal. If you can do it. See, meditation is also painful—both mentally and physically—and in the zendo this becomes abundantly clear.

I barely make it through the first count of one before my attention is diverted by a crow squawking outside. I start to think how all crows sound alike and then, following an imperceptible leap of thought, find myself wondering how silly we all must look sitting on our pillows in semi-darkness. I want to peek around the room but I remember I'm supposed to be counting. *One*, I say, inhaling. *One*, I say, exhaling. *Two*, I say and someone clears his throat. *Hey! Is that legal?* I notice my crotch is starting to burn from the pressure of my body pushing down onto the pillow through the thick seams of my blue jeans. *How can I meditate with a hot crotch?* With grim determination I start counting again and before I know it I've counted to twenty-three while at the same time thinking about the beef burgundy Lezah said she was going to fix for dinner that night. Like ceramic balls on a pool table, my thoughts continue to clack into each other in a wild, geometric search for a dark resting place. About five hours later, or so it seems, the meditation bell rings twice signaling the first round of zazen is at end.

• • •

Several months after my eight-year relationship ended, fate intervened and I met Angela, who is perhaps the most appropriately named person I know. Angela and I started dating and I learned how much her faith in God had guided her life. That's how she talked about it. It was *faith* she possessed. Not religion. Her relationship with God, while shaped by Biblical teaching, was a private matter. She didn't need to follow any sort of decorous ritual in a church to feel holy.

Night after night, in front of fires and over glasses of wine, we talked about Christianity and Jesus and the Bible and how she'd been able to assemble all that into a coherent picture of how God worked in her life. She usually didn't bring up the topic, I did, which enhanced my eagerness to learn. Clearly, *she* wouldn't try to convert me—not that it was something any Joe could do anyway—but she would share whatever information she possessed. Which was a lot. I was deeply impressed, not only by her knowledge, but also by the sense of inner peace she was able to maintain despite her grinding job as a litigator.

Angela's peaceful, private faith confirmed the growing sense I was having that spirituality was, or at least should be, highly individualized. Since we all confront different stones on our paths through life, we shouldn't be expected to use the same guides to navigate around them. We, and maybe I'm just referring to myself here, should be allowed to find the course that works best no matter how patchwork and bizarre that approach may seem to others. If someone wants to meditate in the morning, attend synagogue in the afternoon and not eat meat on Fridays, it shouldn't matter to anyone but the individual who finds comfort in that routine.

Armed with this philosophy, my search for spirituality expanded in new and different ways. I enrolled in a comparative religion class at a local university where a thin, white-bearded professor explained that our earliest exposure to religion forever shapes our perceptions about spiritual matters. For the first time, it made sense why I felt like such a religious outsider.

I interrogated friends about their beliefs and learned, as suspected, that faith tends to be highly personalized. "You mean you talk to God while driving in your *car?*" I asked my friend Dennis. "Is that allowed?"

I started to notice reports in magazines that discussed the science of neurotheology, which claims the human brain is hard-wired to search for spirituality. The research, which suggested that spirituality is an innately human drive, helped me better understand my own seemingly quixotic quest. No wonder I'd spent my life searching. It was in my DNA to do so.

During this period, the religious titles on my bookshelf expanded to include everyone from Saint Augustine and Frederick Buechner to the Dalai Lama and Thich Nhat Hahn. The authors I liked most talked about religion and spirituality as a practice and not as something a person gets once and puts to rest, their soul forever saved, their hearts forever open, their pain forever gone. This gave me hope. With enough time and attention, I was bound to find—at least for a while—that which I sought.

Angela supported my research but routinely cautioned me. "Honey," she said, "you can't *think* your way to faith." She was right, of course. I'd been doing a lot of thinking and decision making about spirituality, but I wasn't actually experiencing any of its benefits. Which is how I came to pursue meditation.

. . .

When the first round of zazen ends, Lezah and I stand and follow the other seminar participants in a slow, walking meditation around the curtained perimeter of the zendo. As I lift one foot and place it on the floor ahead of me, I find myself focusing on how it feels to walk; to shift weight from one foot to the other as the intricate combination of tendons, bone, and muscle work together to support me. I've never paid much attention to my feet before but I'm into it like a baby who's just discovered her toes.

We sit down for the second round of meditation and this time it's easier to control the billiard balls in my brain. I think about breathing. I focus on counting. I feel the cool air that I inhale and the warm air that I exhale and when thoughts about dinner or the cramp in my foot creep in, I push them away and start counting again. It feels good trying not to think. Angela was right: faith and spirituality do come from a different place than the intellect. I think about this until I realize—once again—that I'm not supposed to be thinking. Just when I start to get fidgety, the session ends.

"It was easier that time," I tell Lezah, as we walk back upstairs to the auditorium. She agrees.

We sit down on the wooden seats and the Sensei reappears for his last lecture of the day. As he positions himself on his cushion, I think about the practice of meditation. Although I've tried meditating at home and experienced some of its calming benefits, I've never fully committed myself to daily practice. Maybe this seminar will help me acquire the discipline I need to get to the pillow each day.

The Sensei spends the last hour talking about the practice of Zen. He promises that if we devote ourselves to rigorous daily meditation our lives *will* change. "But this is not an easy path to follow," he cautions, and I believe him. From my own limited experience I know how torturous it can be to sit still and confront the gang members who spray paint my mind with envy, sadness, and the ludicrous-yet-very-real sense that I would be so much happier if only I had larger breasts. The Sensei says focusing our attention on these things allows us to realize how much of our misery is self-generated. Get rid of the self, he reiterates, and you eliminate the suffering.

It's dark outside as Lezah and I get back into the car. Driving home through the lights of downtown Denver, we congratulate ourselves for taking the crucial first step on the path toward regular spiritual practice.

"I'm thinking of creating an altar at home where I can meditate," Lezah says, and goes on to explain how she'd like to commission some original photography for her altar. I pull up in front of her house and am struck by two thoughts: one, that original photography seems like the kind of material attachment Buddhism is supposed to get rid of; and two, I wished I'd thought of it first.

On the twenty minute drive back to my house, I think about Buddhism and how I like what I've learned so far. It doesn't seem to be about morality or ethics. It's not about chasing after God like some Roman charioteer in gold armor. It's not about looking outward for guidance or holiness at all. Instead, it's about looking inward and allowing enlightenment—and whatever concept of God that may entail—come to you. It's different from the seek-and-conquer approach I've been using, and for that reason I'm willing to pursue this path for a while.

But I know it will take time, and that may be the hardest part. As a product of America's fast-food culture, I'm highly accustomed to having my needs met whenever and wherever I want. I can get cash at two in the morning and microwave a four-course meal in minutes. All this conditioning has led me to believe I can improve my life quickly and with minimal effort. But if I've learned anything at all, it's that spirituality doesn't work that way.

I pull into the driveway and shut off the car. I don't know if Buddhism is the spiritual path I will settle on or not, but it feels right to me now, and I do believe that the truffle of wisdom I seek is, if not here, then certainly coming closer. And that just might be enough.

THINKING THE WORST

In early June, I returned from a visit to Asia with the lingering effects of an upper respiratory infection: dry cough, fatigue, and the expectation that I should be excused from all housework.

When the cough remained several weeks later, I decided to visit a doctor. This, in itself, was an accomplishment considering that Angela, like many lawyers, distrusts anyone with a stethoscope. She did her best to discourage me.

"You'd be safer driving on a crowded freeway at a hundred miles an hour than you would be in a doctor's office," she said.

Believing a quick trip down the highway was not what my cough needed, I kept the appointment.

Waiting for the doctor, I casually leafed through *People*. I wasn't worried about my diagnosis. I merely needed some strong antibiotics to trample the exotic travel bug I'd acquired. Or so I assumed.

The doctor took me into his office and asked questions about my health, family history, travels, and lifestyle. He seemed impressed that I wrote for a living. "You know all those big words," he said. I wasn't sure which big words he was referring to but I was fairly certain none of the big words I knew compared to his lexicon of medical terms.

After a preliminary exam, he sent me down the hall for a chest X-ray. Twenty minutes later, I'm back in his office, standing in front of a lightboard, reviewing the silvery, black-and-white images of my lungs. He points to a ghostly, irregular circle about the size of a nickel and says in his best casual-doctor voice: "Everything on your X-ray looks normal except for this... *lesion.*"

I didn't hear what he said immediately after that because the word "lesion" was echoing around my brain: lesion...sion... sion. It was not a cheerful echo, but rather like the sound of God warning Noah of a prolonged period of rain...ain...ain.

Before I knew what was happening, the doctor's assistants were drawing tubes of blood from my left arm, administering tuberculosis tests to my right arm, scheduling CT scans, and arranging for me to visit a pulmonary specialist. My official diagnosis was "cavitary nodule," which are two big words that I personally have never used.

Arriving back home, I immediately logged onto the Internet to see what this cavitary nodule might indicate. Tuberculosis was a definite possibility. But as I scanned web pages managed by such esteemed groups as the World Health Organization and the Mayo Clinic, it became clear—or at least as clear as it could be in my state of fear-fueled ignorance—that my symptoms could also be caused by a host of other deadly diseases. At best, my nodule would require a protracted period of chemotherapy. More likely, I'd be in an iron lung by Christmas.

Somehow, I made it through two week's worth of medical appointments and the test results came in. Bloodwork? Normal. TB test? Negative. CT scan? Clear. I didn't know whether to be elated over the good results or worried that I'd contracted a new more elusive disease. After all, there was that lesion-sion-sion to contend with.

A week later, while standing with a short, serious, bow-tied pulmonologist in front of my X-ray, he says to me: "Hmmmm...you seem healthy in all other respects. I'd like you to take another X-ray and this time I'd like you to wear a couple of markers."

Puzzled, I marched back down the hall to X-ray and told the technician what the doctor had said. Soon, I found myself taping two tiny metal ball bearings to the same parts of my anat omy that The Millionaire Bride had recently bared in *Playboy* magazine.

The films were taken again and the ball-bearing images told us what we needed to know: I didn't have a lesion after all. Instead, and this is a word I've never used in print before, I had an unusually photogenic nipple. What can I say? It was cold in the X-ray room.

My cough was not caused by tuberculosis or cancer. Instead, as suspected, it was the stubborn result of a respiratory infection, and thanks to medication, it is now almost gone. My lesion, as it were, had simply misled my medical team.

Driving home, I searched for the lesson behind the lesion. Was this a warning against the perils of self-diagnosis? A reminder to dress warmly at the doctor's office? Maybe neither. Or both. Or maybe I wasn't supposed to know. Maybe I was supposed to learn to stop jumping to so many premature conclusions and wait for all the facts of a situation to present themselves.

I called Angela on the phone to tell her I didn't have a lesion after all. "I have a nipple," I said.

The line clicked softly for a moment. And then Angela responded, calmly, with a great deal of lawyerly restraint: "*I* could have told you that." ❖

The Gift of Envy

The summer I was twenty years old, I worked as a maid at the Sahara Tahoe Hotel and Casino. My uniform consisted of an orange-and-blue plaid smock like those worn by pretzel vendors at major league football games. The smock was matched with a pair of dark blue polyester pants with a thick elastic waistband and crotch that hung to mid-thigh. It was a uniform custom fit for pregnant maids, or maids with extremely short legs. I was neither.

If I rolled up the waistband to adjust the crotch, the pants rose to mid-calf exposing white legs and short dark socks. If I left the waistband as it was, the long crotch caused me to walk as if I had braces on my legs. In retrospect, I realize the job was one of those life-changing events that woke me up to the value of a college education. But at the time, I was too distracted by envy.

You see, I had applied at the hotel along with a number of women I knew from college. After my application was processed, I was handed a pair of yellow rubber gloves and instructed on the importance of creating triangular "courtesy folds" on the rolls of toilet paper in each guest bathroom. "At the Sahara Tahoe, these details *matter*," the trainer explained with an earnestness that far outstripped the subject matter.

Two of my friends, however, were granted vastly different assignments. One, a blonde beauty straight off the set of a forties film noir, was hired as a lifeguard. Another was hired as the pool's cocktail waitress. Both of them were named Karen.

Every day from my perch inside the guestrooms on the upper

floors, I could see the Karens "working" in the sun alongside the hotel's large blue pool. Gripping a toilet brush in one hand, a wastebasket in the other, I felt like the mongrel puppy at an animal shelter that has to compete with purebred Collies for adoption. Even the two-dollar tip I occasionally plucked from used pillowcases didn't alleviate my deep-seated envy.

Of course, at the time, I rationalized my employment situation in the most mature way I knew how: "I'm too fair skinned to be a lifeguard and not slutty enough to be a cocktail waitress."

Sadly, my jealously over the Karens was not an isolated event. Envy is something I've battled ever since I entered the work world, although it often lurks—at least for a while—behind other emotions.

I listen to accomplished writers at bookstore readings and comment, with the thin-lipped superiority of a *New York Times* book critic, about how the writer wasn't *that* funny, or how unfortunate it was that her last three books didn't sell as well as the first.

I learn about a thirteen-year-old art prodigy who's commanding six figures for original oils and state, with Freudian concern, how tragic it is she doesn't have time for hopscotch.

Sometimes, though, the envy is more apparent.

For example, I recently learned that a cousin, now in his mid-thirties, had just masterminded his second takeover of an ailing pharmaceutical company. All I could think about was how lamentable it was that my resume didn't boast a single corporate takeover.

Among the many other professionals I've envied are, in no particular order, jailhouse ministers, symphony conductors, playwrights, art house auctioneers, and anthropology professors. I've also found myself wishing I could be more like people who wear loud clothing or sport colorful tattoos. (Just for the record, I have never envied politicians or accountants.)

For a time I thought my chronic sense of envy was the result of a basic dissatisfaction with my own career choices. But several years ago, I came to realize that envy is so much more than insecurity.

On September 11, 2001, I sat riveted to television footage of New York City firefighters clawing their way through the rubble that was once the World Trade Center. As I watched them working covered with sweat, grime and unspeakable grief, I thought about the truly important work firefighters do; I envied their commitment and determination, their bravery and sense of civic duty. I wondered if I were too old to become a firefighter, completely overlooking the fact that I'm a wuss who's scared of both fire and heights.

Watching the firefighters in their yellow slickers, I wondered: perhaps envy is not solely the result of insecurity or unhappiness. Perhaps it's also about admiration. Perhaps we envy people because they exhibit qualities, traits, and abilities that matter to us, abilities we wish we had more of, abilities we work to develop.

Thinking back to when I was twenty, I envied the Karens because they set out to get fun jobs that summer, while I simply took what was available.

The writers I've most envied are those who write with brilliance and are disciplined enough to complete whole novels year after year.

And I envied my cousin because he's young, smart as a firecracker, and goal-minded—all of which are qualities I wish I had more of.

Especially youth.

And smarts.

In fact, when I think about it, I admire success, public service, artistry, loyalty, confidence, and devotion in any form, and the people I've envied most are those who exhibit those qualities in spades.

Now, whenever I feel the sickening knife-twist of envy, I don't automatically assume it's because I've accomplished less than I think I'm able. Instead, I try to see what it is I admire about the person I envy. In a sense, the people I'm most jealous of are those who can plug me back into my own value system and remind me about the characteristics and behaviors that I find important.

The writers, artists, firefighters, and cocktail waitresses in my life have all given me a tremendous gift: the gift of envy. Now, if I can only teach them about the vital importance of triangular courtesy folds.

LOOKING FOR LACY

The only advice I have about dating and college is this: If you're flat-chested and insecure, acquire a voluptuous roommate who speaks Italian, paints her fingernails black, and thinks you're just amusing enough to bring along to parties where you'll meet drama majors, women who smoke long brown cigarettes, and dark-haired men who use phrases like "last weekend's lover" without any hint of shame or self-consciousness.

I was blessed with such a roommate. Her name was Lacy and she was car-stopping gorgeous: minty green eyes, olive skin, and brown hair as thick and long as a European princess. Lacy could have sex anytime she wanted with men she actually wanted to see again the next day.

Lacy and I lived together in a motel-style apartment during our junior year at California State University. During that year, we'd go to parties at the foreign language house near campus, and after several tumblers of cheap red wine, we'd dance together and kiss, closed-mouthed, like French girlfriends. This made us feel worldly, like two mature women without sexual boundaries. In truth, she was the worldly one; I was merely faking it in an effort to impress her. Like a shy student who offers to clean the blackboards after class, I yearned to be Lacy's chosen pupil.

I haven't seen Lacy in almost twenty years and I'm on a quest to find her, not only to see if her smile and sophistication remain intact, but also because I have something to return to her. Something that is the embodiment of youth, life, and possibility. And no, I'm not referring to the *Fame* soundtrack she and I played every single afternoon for an entire semester. I'm talking about the return of her memories.

Let me explain.

The summer we graduated, I took a public relations job at the local chamber of commerce primarily because it was the only job offered to me. However, Lacy—in a classic uber-sophisticate move—announced she was going to Venice.

"In *Italy?*" I asked, believing Italy to be about as foreign and far away a person could get and still wear shoes.

"Yes, Italy," she said, tapping the ash from her Virginia Slims into an empty black espresso cup. At the time, the closest I'd ever gotten to Italy were the yellowing photos of gondoliers that hung on the walnut-paneled walls of a family-run pasta restaurant near my house. I couldn't fathom how a person could just *go* to Venice. Didn't you need paperwork? Clearances? Money? "I'll be living with a family and working on my Italian," she said, as if that explained everything.

Several months later, we sat across from each other in my one-bedroom apartment with the shag carpet and olive-green refrigerator and she told me about her experiences. What I recall most is not how happy Lacy was to have spent a long summer sipping *caffe freddo* and dipping her toes into the Grand Canal. Instead, I recall her rocking slowly back and forth in my wooden rocker, staring at the floor, and talking about how much she'd changed.

"How so?" I asked.

"I'm not sure. I just feel different." This alarmed me because Lacy was different but she always appeared completely at ease in most situations. If grown-up adventures like travel made confident people like Lacy unsure of herself, what hope was there for the rest of us?

"Why don't you write about your experiences?" I suggested. "A summer in Venice sounds like a great short story. Maybe even a novel."

"But you're the writer," she said.

I reminded her that my literary experience had been limited to newsletter articles about ribbon cuttings at local hair salons. "Besides," I added. "I didn't go to Italy. You did."

Suddenly, Lacy stopped rocking and leaned forward in her chair. "What if I gave you my journal from the trip?" she asked, her green eyes alive for the first time that evening. "Would you be willing to read it and write a story about my experience?"

My thoughts raced back to the first time I read *Playboy* magazine while babysitting for the mailman's family down the street. In a house filled with hook rugs and empty baby bottles there existed a bookcase where the bottom two shelves were crammed with *Playboys* dating back years. The glossy, full-color photography introduced me to a world so forbidden yet so titillating that I'd been forced by the raw power of adolescent sexuality to conduct strip-tease dances for the twelve-year-old girl next door, who'd selflessly volunteered to babysit with me. I imagined Lacy's diary would be equally thrilling. So I agreed.

The next day Lacy came by my office and handed me a paper bag containing a journal covered in a flowery, dark blue fabric, three sixty-minute cassette tapes sent to her in Italy by her boyfriend, and six letters that she'd mailed home to her family. I took Lacy's bag of memories home, poured a glass of wine, and jotted some writerly notes about what kind of tale this might become. A romance? Coming of age? Travelogue? I was hyped by the challenge of unraveling the mystery of Lacy's Italian summer.

As it turned out, unraveling the mysteries of my own life at twenty-two proved far more alluring. Instead of reading her diary, I chose to write rambling, marijuana-induced entries into my own diary. Entries that typically began with the word "why" and ended with three overwrought question marks followed by an enormous doodle involving seagulls. Consequently, like all writing projects I contemplated in my twenties, Lacy's story eventually became nothing more than another dusty addition to the hope chest of good intentions.

A year after Lacy gave me her journal, I changed jobs, packed her memories into a cardboard box that once held Sara Lee homestyle pies, and moved from my apartment into a house. That same box has since accompanied me on three moves in California, one long U-Haul trip across the Rockies, and four moves in Colorado. It now rests on the dark lower shelf of my office closet. It's been almost twenty years and I've neither read, nor written, a single word about Lacy's experience. I also haven't spoken to the journal's author since she gave it to me on that gray winter day in northern California in 1983. She moved south, I stayed north, and the pull of young adult life proved stronger than our friendship.

I now want to find my old roommate, not only to determine if I've caught up with her sophistication-wise. After all, I've now been to Europe, oh, let's see, what is it? *Six* times already? I also want to find Lacy because I now think it's bad juju to hold on to someone else's personal mementos for so long. I didn't come to this conclusion without help. An ex-lover has been holding some of my photographs hostage for eight years now and I'm a bit peeved about it. It's not that I'm all that eager to look at photos of myself in a perm and gold-rimmed aviator glasses. I just don't want anybody else to either. A person's younger self and all the attendant embarrassments should rightfully remain with its owner.

There is one other reason I want to return the journal: If Lacy's anything like me—not that she ever was—she may be waxing nostalgic for those halcyon days of young adulthood when life brimmed with possibility and the grooves of daily life were not so deeply worn they were impossible to crawl out of. Not that I personally know anyone who feels this way, of course. I just think it would be gratifying to re-establish contact with someone who made such a deep impression on my own barely formed grooves half a lifetime ago. I'm not sure why talking to Lacy has come to seem so important, but I sense it has to do with growing older and finding that true friendships are harder to come by the older I get. Perhaps I'm not ready to close the chapter on an old friend until I know what happened to her. But where to begin?

The only unconfirmed information I have is that Lacy once taught aerobics in Dallas, and may have married a black weatherman in New York City. Both seem plausible, but it's not much to go on. I log onto the Internet, type her name into the Google search engine and get nowhere in a hurry. I then search for several hours on Yahoo, the international online white pages, and California State University's alumni database. Lacy remains elusive.

I remove her letters from the Sara Lee box and notice her family's home address in Southern California. When we were in college, I once accompanied Lacy on a visit home. She was from a large, Italian Catholic family and had something like fifty-seven older brothers and sisters. Two of them might have been named Maria. I recall following Lacy down a long narrow hallway, off of which were countless bedrooms with two and three and four beds apiece. It wasn't a home as much as a well-organized dormitory with enormous silver pots hanging in the kitchen and a washing machine that never stopped rumbling. Wondering if her family still lives there, I type the name and address into the search engine and discover that, indeed, a Leigh remains in the ancestral home. Armed with a name and address, finding the phone number should be a snap. And surely, whoever answers the phone will know how to find Lacy. But am I really ready to contact her?

I pick up Lacy's dark blue, fabric-covered journal and open it. The spine cracks and a chunk of yellowing pages separate from the dried-glue binding and drop onto my desk. It's as if all those years of waiting in the closet have caused the journal to lose patience. Clearly, it *wants* to be read. At least that's what I tell myself for I am now inexplicably seized by the desire to read about Lacy's experience. Is it nosiness? Probably. But is also seems somewhat disrespectful to return the journal without having read a word of it. Calling her can wait.

I open the journal to the first page. It's dated: 6/11/82. *"I didn't sleep at all the night before I took off..."*

I read the first few pages and learn that Lacy lived with an older married couple in a small second-story duplex on the Lido di Venezia, an island of thirty-thousand residents across the water from Venice. She slept on a twin bed that had been pushed up against a wall in the family's dining room. As I read, I picture Lacy in a long white nightgown, sitting on a knobby bedspread underneath a gold-framed picture of the Virgin Mary. She's painting her toenails and the blue journal rests on the bed next to her. Outside, young people can be heard bicycling home from their jobs in Venice where they've spent the day selling pigeon food to tourists at St. Mark's Square. While waiting for the polish to dry, Lacy picks up the journal to record her day.

The first couple of weeks, she writes about loneliness, jet lag and adjusting to a new routine where lunch—*pranzo*—consists of five large courses all washed down with a bottle of cold white wine. She also longs for her boyfriend. *"God, I miss him,"* she writes. *"I hope I get a letter soon."* She ends each entry with the salutation, *"Buona notte!"*

At first, it feels voyeuristic to be reading someone else's journal, like watching an older woman undress through a backyard window and discovering she wears panties with frayed lace. Journals are private spaces designed to remain that way.

But I remind myself that Lacy gave me permission to read her words. She invited me to enter her thoughts and have a look around. And so I do. And soon, I become so captivated in the routine of Lacy's life in Italy that I no longer sense I'm reading about her experiences; I feel like I'm experiencing them for myself.

As she searches for gifts for her family, I can picture myself peering through small shop windows at a jumble of merchandise where everything is marked in the thousands of lira.

As she struggles to get along with her host, I can feel the teeth-grinding frustration of not being able to communicate in the same language.

When she goes on a premenstrual eating binge and in one six-hour period devours an ice cream cone, a bag of biscotti, a chunk of chocolate with hazelnuts, two more ice cream cones, and dinner followed by milk and cookies, I recall all the times I've succumbed to the allure of sugar or alcohol or pot or sex.

Before I know it, I'm reflecting back on my own experiences at twenty-two and wondering why the hell I didn't go to Italy, or even Los Angeles. Why did I stay in my northern California college town and take the first job offered? At twenty-two, Lacy was drinking wine—at lunch—and spending afternoons at the beach reading the Italian edition of *Cosmopolitan*. What made her so different then?

I read on, looking for clues in Lacy's handwritten journal entries. Her handwriting is so familiar. It's neat, but not obsessively so, with just the right amount of stylistic flourish. As I turn the pages, I begin to notice that unlike my younger self, Lacy didn't consume much paper pondering Life's Big Questions. Although at the end of her European sojourn she would be going home to find a job, she mentions the uncertainty of her future only once. Instead, as her journal makes clear, she was living life from the middle of it. *"I learned a new verb tense last night!"* she writes in early July. *"Now, jokes make so much more sense!"*

But what happened in Italy to make Lacy feel so different and uncertain several months later? If she didn't go to Italy with questions, why did she return with them? I continue to read and slowly realize that reading about someone's life on a daily basis is not as captivating or revealing as it might sound. Life rarely changes in dramatic, sweepstakes-winner fashion. Instead, most of the changes we experience occur through small cellular-level divisions that are only noticeable only after considerable time has passed.

To be sure, there were high points in Lacy's trip. She had an affair with a man who was thirteen years older and a part-time gondolier, or so he claimed. She had a passionate afternoon on

the beach with a dental student, passionate being my euphe-
mistically chosen adjective for an encounter she describes over
the course of several pages with words like "horny," "outra-
geously wonderful," and "the biggest I've ever seen."

Despite these romps, Lacy continued to promise, in dou-
ble-underlined script, to remain faithful to her boyfriend back
home. *"We both agreed to take surrogate lovers, if necessary,"* she
writes. To this day, Lacy is the only person I know who can use
a term like "surrogate lover" and get away with it. So if these
affairs weren't life-changing for her, what was?

I read her journal clear to the end where the last image pre-
sented is one of Lacy smoking a cigarette while sitting at a
gate in the Zurich airport. She's waiting for her parents and
several siblings to arrive so they can travel together throughout
southern Europe before she returns home for good. *"I was re-
reading some of what I'd written in the beginning of my stay,"* she
writes on the last page. *"Sure is different than how I feel now."*

I don't get it. What change had befallen her? How was she
different? I now know what Lacy's experience in Italy had been.
But the story, at least that which is obvious from her journal, is still missing. The crime has not been solved and I can't
return her mementos until I know what happened.

Searching for additional insight, I listen to her boyfriend's
tapes. He talks slowly, and spends an excessive amount of time
talking about his stereo equipment and how the red and green
level lights rise and fall with the sound of his voice. Like wow,
man. The first two tapes consist mostly of him playing the
guitar and making up songs with lyrics like, *I make one and you
make two/ a groove times two/ I love you.*

By the third tape, however, her boyfriend confesses that he is
feeling differently about life, and I start to glimpse the change
Lacy may have been referring to upon her return. The gist of
his last, sixty minute tape is this: "We need to talk about our
expectations for our reunion... I don't want illusions of a
grand romance...My life is world's away from where it was..."
Ultimately, near the end of the tape, he records these words:

"I'm involved in another relationship." Apparently, he didn't take the 'surrogate' part of their arrangement as seriously as Lacy had. Being dumped by Memorex at the end of a summer in Venice had to have been, as we said back then, "a bummer."

But today, twenty years later, I choose not to believe that Lacy was despondent in my apartment on that cold winter day because she'd been dumped. By a guy. I choose to believe there was more to her transformation in Italy than could be understood just a few months later. Not enough time had passed to give Lacy the perspective she needed to make sense of her experience. I push her journal and letters and tapes to the side of my desk. I need to find Lacy, and find out how she now interprets her summer in Venice.

As I pick up the phone to dial her parent's number, I think what my objectives are for the phone call. One, I'd like to know what Lacy's done with her life over the past two decades. Two, I'd like to know if she's still as glamorous as I remember, or if maybe she's gotten a teensy bit fat. Three, I want an ending to this story. I want to know how Italy transformed her and how a summer abroad changes the course of a young woman's life. Her mother answers on the third ring and tells me Lacy is now living just two miles away. I hang up and punch in Lacy's number before I can chicken out. She answers with the same warm seductive voice I remember.

"Shari?" she says, after I introduce myself. "You're kidding? What prompted you to call?"

Suddenly, I feel stupid prying into Lacy's life, like there is so little going on in my own that I have to vicariously experience someone else's life from twenty years ago to have a little fun. "I'll tell you in a minute," I say, in an effort to buy time. "What've you been up to?"

I learn that Lacy entered the fitness business upon her return from Italy and was on the leading edge of the aerobics industry for years. Yes, she lived in Dallas for a time. Yes, she also lived in New York, where she was a sought-after personal trainer for such celebrities as Whoopi Goldberg and Brooke Shields.

Brooke *Shields*, I think to myself. The only celebrities in my past are fitness guru Jack LaLanne, for whom I once organized a press conference, and Rich Little, the impressionist, with whom I once shared an elevator. Lacy continues talking and I learn that she didn't marry a black weatherman after all. She married a Jewish lawyer.

"A Jew?" I ask, thinking of all the times in her journal where she mentioned visiting cathedrals and lighting candles.

"Yeah, you know, I always was the family rebel. Not only did I stop going to Catholic church, but I also married a Heeb." We talk for several more minutes and I learn she recently returned to Southern California, has three small children and a nanny, and continues her personal training business part-time. "So tell me, Shari, what made you call me after all this time?"

My mouth starts to feel all pasty and I find myself reluctant to tell her that I've been reading her most intimate thoughts of twenty years ago. I'm beginning to feel like a stalker, like she's David Letterman and I'm that woman who used to sleep by his tennis courts and go through his garbage and drive his Porsche. What was I thinking? That I could just call someone out of the blue and ask her what a summertime experience meant because I needed an ending to a story? Well, yes, come to think of it, that *was* what I was thinking. And although part of me wants to quietly hang up the phone and tiptoe out of my office, the part that wants to know how she interprets her summer wins out.

"Remember when you returned from Venice twenty years ago?" I ask.

"Yes," she says slowly.

"Remember when you gave me your journal from the trip? And your boyfriend's tapes? And your letters home to your parents?"

"I *did?*" she replies. "I wondered where those things went."

This is worse than I thought it would be. She doesn't even remember giving me the journal let alone giving me permission to write about her experiences.

"Yeah, ha ha, you gave them to me and told me to write a story about your summer."

Her end of the line is silent.

"Well, I just read them."

More silence.

"And I'm writing something. And. Um. Can I ask you a few questions."

"Okaaaay," she replies.

I plunge onward. I ask Lacy what she remembers most about that summer. I ask what the experience meant to her. I ask how Italy changed her.

"Are you interviewing me?" she asks, with a slight laugh. I'm not sure whether the laugh is out of nervousness or designed to let me know my questions are okay. I hear a little girl cry in the background.

"Yeah, I guess I am interviewing you."

"I haven't thought about that summer in a long time you know, but the experience was definitely life-altering."

Well, duh, I think to myself. I knew that twenty years ago. "How so?" I prod.

"It was really growthful," she explains. "I became so much more independent. And I learned long-distance relationships don't last."

I raise my eyes and lean forward in an encouraging but skeptical way, the way Diane Sawyer does when she's trying to get a celebrity to reveal an affair. Of course, Lacy can't see this posture, but it makes me feel better. I'm just about to ask another question when Lacy changes the conversation to 9-11, to the people we knew in college, and to how happy she'll be to send family photos over the Internet. "But I really have to go now," she says. "My kids are getting restless."

I hang up the phone feeling not only stupid, but disappointed.

I desperately wanted Lacy to reveal some awe-inspiring connection between her summer in Venice and her life afterward. I wanted a direct cause-and-effect relationship that might compel me to take the summer off and flee to Italy. I wanted a neat

Hollywood ending where the dental student on the beach is connected to the Jew in New York and the big mid-day *pranzos* evolve into a life-long zeal for fitness. Cut. Print. Roll the credits. But I didn't get any of those neat connections and it may be because Lacy's been living her life, not editing it into some kind of epic tale with moral lessons for lesser humans.

I pick up Lacy's journal, finger the dry paper edges and realize that has always been her approach to life. In college, while I was busy fretting about how to become more seductive, Lacy exuded sensuality. While I spent time processing failed relationships over plates of Mexican food, she was busy creating new ones. From the very first day I knew her, Lacy seemed able to seize life without the burden of questions that have often seized me in my tracks. And it's still that way. I wanted to know how Lacy had changed and her lack of a response was the most appropriate one she could give.

I put Lacy's journal and letters and cassette tapes into a small box and search for an address label. Connecting with her and reflecting on the past twenty years has taught me that we're not frozen in time like mosquitoes in amber. We eat. We travel. We have sex, sometimes in Italian. And life progresses whether we stop to obsess about it or not.

WHY WE WORK

My twelve year old niece Taylor thinks I'm way cooler than her mom because I know everything there is to know about everything. The other day, in her quest to take advantage of my vast knowledge, she asked: "Auntie Shari, why do people like to work?"

Immediately, I was suspicious. "*Like* to work, dearheart? Who's been filling your pretty young head with such thoughts?"

"Well," she replied, "every now and then I hear grown-ups say things like 'I had a great day at work.' What makes work great? I thought because it was called work it wasn't supposed to be fun."

And that's when I realized what an opportunity I had. I could talk to Taylor about fancy titles and fat bonuses and fashionable offices and the other things that are supposed to make work great. Instead, I chose to tell her about the many other reasons people go to work each day and find it enjoyable.

What I told her was this:

"We work because we like the inky smell inside a new box of business cards printed with our name and title.

"We work because we like giving presentations that provide an excuse to buy the expensive black suit before it goes on sale.

"We work for the satisfaction of helping someone less experienced learn how to close a sale or write a brief or transfer an elderly patient from one bed to another.

"We work because we enjoy going to conferences and wearing plastic name badges that show we're part of professions we care about.

"We work to make our parents proud, even if we're fully grown and our parents have already told us a gazillion times how proud they are.

"We work to make our kids proud, if not today, then someday when they're old enough to understand we're not total geeks.

"We work for those Sally Field moments when we realize that our boss and co-workers and clients like us. They *really, really* like us."

"Who's Sally Field?" Taylor asked.

"She's a famous actress," I explained.

"Like Mary-Kate and Ashley?"

"Sort of. You see, Taylor, I don't think we work because we like getting up at six, grabbing a breakfast bar, and putting on makeup while stuck in rush hour traffic. But we do like being needed and having deadlines and whenever we forget that, we talk to retired people who are wistful for the days when they were a part of things.

"We work because we like going into an office we've made all our own with color photos, a Zen rock garden, and a yellow stuffed Tweety Bird that says, *Yoo hoo, poody tat,* when you hit its fuzzy little head.

"We work because there's nothing cooler than checking e-mail in the morning and finding a note from someone we last saw at a Bee Gees concert in 1978.

"We work for those moments when people we've never met compliment us on our work.

"We work for the thrill of beating a deadline everyone thought was impossible.

"We work because we like becoming experts in subjects other people don't know about. Things like how to write an annual report, or program a computer, or fix a broken leg.

"We don't go to work because we like office politics or stress or having to refill the coffee pot every morning because no one else will. We go to work because we've learned how to get a smile out of Ed in the mailroom, or because Kyndra the receptionist laughs at our jokes, or because we've learned something titillating about Myra in finance and she doesn't know that we know.

"We work because every single good friend we've made over the last twenty years has come about through work associations.

"Most of all, we work because every one of us, in some way, believes our work is important to others."

Taylor looked up at me, her face gleaming with adoration. "You mean to tell me that people don't work simply because they want to make more money for Microsoft or Proctor and Gamble or Wal-Mart?" she asked.

I smiled at her thinking how much she was becoming like her favorite aunt. "Some people do," I responded, "because it provides a feeling of accomplishment."

Taylor thought about this for a moment. "But based on what you said, it seems that people work for other, more personal reasons—reasons like friendship and accomplishment and affiliation and ownership. It seems to me that people work to fulfill their own needs first and the company's needs second."

My smile grew. I obviously had a prodigy on my hands. Taylor continued: "Maybe if more companies understood what makes work *fun* for people they would be able to create more fulfilling and more profitable workplaces."

"Sounds good to me," I responded.

"But wait, I have one more question: What do you know about Myra in the finance department?"

"I'll never tell."

Pee Here Now

Several years ago, I switched health insurance companies and my new insurer sent a uniformed nurse with short black hair to my house to conduct a health assessment. We sat at my kitchen table and she officiously asked questions about my health history.

"Diabetes?" she asked, as if accusing me of illicit drug use. "No," I answered. "Cancer?" Nope. "High blood pressure?" Nope.

When she'd completed the questionnaire, she reached into a portable metal case and retrieved a white plastic cup. "Last thing I'll need is a urine sample," she said, sliding the cup toward me across the wooden table.

I took the cup to my bathroom, set it on the white tile counter, unzipped my jeans, sat down, and promptly started thinking about something else. Many long seconds later, I stood, re-zipped my jeans, and, still absorbed in my thoughts, looked down to find the empty plastic cup waiting on the tile counter.

My consciousness careened back to the present. The cup! How could I forget to fill the cup? I picked it up and held it at eye level. The cup seemed larger somehow, and infinitely unfillable, like a gigantic movie prop from *Honey, I Shrunk the Kids.* I set it back down and considered my options.

I could fill the cup with water and "trip" on my way out of the bathroom. I could invent an excuse involving dehydration or bladder shyness. I could wedge through the narrow window above the bathtub and flee to the airport.

Realizing none of these schemes would work, I ultimately

had to admit to the nurse that I'd forgotten what I'd gone to the bathroom for. "I can drink a bunch of water and try again in a few minutes," I offered.

"That's okay," she said, grabbing the empty cup and dropping it into her metal box. "I'll come back tomorrow. I have nothing better to do."

I'd like to report this was an aberrant bout of absent-mindedness, something that could be chalked up to cold medication or a fight with my mother. But the fact is, I tend to forget. A lot. And it's getting worse.

In the last several months, I've left my purse in two Mexican restaurants, a coffee shop, the trunk of a friend's car, and a department store dressing room. Two weeks ago, I removed a nozzle from my garden hose and spent the latter part of that afternoon trying, in vain, to discover where I'd placed it.

The scary part for me is that over the last few months I've also been going to a Zen Center in an effort to practice meditation and mindfulness. One of my goals has been to become less forgetful by being more fully present. Or, to paraphrase a popular Buddhist saying, "To pee here now." But I've even forgotten things at the Zen Center, like the time I misplaced my purse before an important ceremony and had nothing to contribute to the fight against world hunger.

The increasing bouts of absent-mindedness had been worrying me, and the jokes from friends about early Alzheimer's were starting to be not so hilarious. But last week I got some valuable insight into absent-mindedness when I completed an assessment called the Gregorc Style Delineator.

This assessment groups people into four types based on how they value certain words. The word *lively*, for example, struck me as more appealing than *rational*. I liked *spontaneous* better than *troubleshooter*.

When the results of my word valuations were tabulated, I was shown to be a clear "Abstract Random," whose negative characteristics include a proclivity towards "flightiness," and an inattention to detail which often earns them the title of—

and I'm quoting directly from the assessment—"an off-the-wall flake."

However, in reviewing the assessment, I learned there are several good reasons why Abstract Randoms—"ARs" for short—appear so flighty. For starters, and I'm bragging only a little here, ARs have vivid imaginations, a tremendous capacity to absorb and relate seemingly unrelated facts, and they often divert their attention only to that which has personal meaning. (A urine cup? I don't *think* so.) Furthermore, ARs rarely work in a sterile office with an orderly desk. Instead, and I plead guilty, the office of an AR is located in whatever coffee shop she happens to be working in. Her filing cabinet is in her head.

Needless to say, I found these results reassuring. As a journalist, I'm paid to find connections between people and the events that surround them. Thus, I have to spend time musing about life and what it means, and sometimes the best time for musing is when I'm doing some other mindless task. So what if I forget a purse in the process?

All of this has gotten me to thinking about something I learned in a novel writing class: A character's greatest strength is also her biggest weakness. It's certainly true in my case, but it's also true of many people: the brilliant physician who focuses so intently on healing a patient's body that he neglects to comfort her soul; the quick-thinking marketing whiz who's hugely intolerant of people who don't "get it" as quickly as he does. Even Einstein, from what I hear, couldn't remember his own address or phone number.

The point I'm trying to make, and I'm not at all defensive about this, is that no one is strong in all facets of human behavior. Some of us are good with people, others with data; some are logical, others reactive; some pay attention, others...

What were we talking about? Anyway, chances are, the better you are at one end of the spectrum, the worse you'll be at the other. How many visual artists do you know who could run an accounting firm?

Instead of judging a person's weaknesses, wouldn't it be kinder to recognize her strengths and offer to drive her to the restaurant where she left her car keys the night before? I think so.

How To Rent a Video

Selecting a proper video for home viewing is a methodical process, one that requires careful forethought and an abundance of tactical maneuvering. One cannot, should not, embark on the video selection process blithely, even though the suggestion—"Hey! Let's rent a video!"—sounds so cheerily innocuous. It's not. It's an invitation to social collapse.

To avoid this, you must carefully choose your viewing companions and employ different selection tactics based on the target audience.

Your Parents

Let's say your parents are visiting from far away. With them, you probably shouldn't even suggest watching a video. After all, they've traveled all this way—bad hip, arthritis and all—to visit with you. They didn't fly here to watch a video. They can watch a video any old day. But since you moved so far away and rarely come home for a visit and hardly ever call, well, wouldn't you just prefer to sit down and talk like a real family? Talking is nice. People never talk anymore.

"We want to know what's going on in your life," your mother says, "and what it is you've done to your hair."

So you sit down, pour yourself a gin and tonic with a weency bit more gin than usual, and commence to talking because you realize that watching a video is not an acceptable form of visiting with your parents.

Unless, of course, they break the three-day rule.

If your parents remain in your home expecting your stellar hospitality to continue after three days of relentless visiting, you are completely within your rights as a fully functioning adult human being with no lingering childhood issues to suggest renting a video.

But nothing with sex in it. And no subtitles. Your father hates subtitles. He's never actually *seen* a movie with subtitles, but he knows this instinctively. Like he knows he would not enjoy carrying a man purse, or eating meat with grilled fruit.

Of course, your mother would welcome a light romantic comedy. But your father requires a good war epic. The ideal compromise would be something along the lines of *Pretty Woman* meets *Schindler's List*. You discuss the possibilities with them over dinner.

Your mother agrees with every suggestion you make because she's come all this way and she's working hard to make sure you two have a memorable visit. Your father, however, is not similarly compelled. He decides he's tired and what he'd really like to do is go to bed. Which he does.

And as you watch him walk upstairs, your mother turns to you and says: "We can watch a movie next time, honey. I promise."

Smart Couples

You're dining at a restaurant with a married couple you admire for their education and success and willingness to delve inside any conversational topic. You've planned to "grab a video" on the way home and watch it together. So, over dessert, you start talking about the latest movies. Only these particular friends don't watch movies. They watch *films*.

They watch foreign films about dead composers and tortured artists and thin women who live lonely lives in small apartments with dead spider plants. They describe these films as "emotionally brutal," "uncompromisingly bleak," and "masterpieces of human misery, madness, and misanthropy."

They talk about writers and directors like they vacationed with them in Greece just last week. "Spielberg is so tired of Hollywood these days." "The Coen brothers? What cards." You think these friends might be pretentious but you overlook it because they like you.

So you start to suggest films to rent. But before you can say *Bruce Almighty*, they've already decided on the perfect selection. It's a Czech film, they say; a film that is Just So You. A film that is so grand and engrossing and allegorical that they wouldn't mind watching it again even though they've already seen in three times. "Really," they argue. "We wouldn't mind. At. All."

They don't actually say this but it's clear your appalling lack of culture and sophistication is at stake. As ambassadors for the cultural elite, this very smart couple is willing to sacrifice on your behalf and you darn well better appreciate it.

"A Czech film," you say. "Sounds great."

Young Children

This is a particularly vexing category of viewership. On the one hand, whenever you get the chance to watch movies with children—say, your young nieces—you want to indulge them. You want to be known as the Favorite Aunt. The Cool Grownup. You want to let them watch *The Lion King* and *Snow White* and *Pocahontas*, even if they already know all the words and insist on telling you every three minutes about the great scene that is coming up.

"This next part is where Simba wanders off on his own and it's soooo sad," they say. They relay this information slowly, because they know you know you have limited Lion King experience and it may be challenging for you to fully grasp the emotional nuance of this epic tale.

The scene ends and you agree it was very sad, but your nieces tell you to be quiet because the scary part with the hyenas is next.

"And then after that," they say, "Simba meets with Timon and Pumbaa."

"And then after that," they say, "they sing *Hakuna Matata.*"

You listen in a drooling stupor until everyone in the room has stopped singing, at which point you decide being the favorite aunt is no longer important. You now want to be a good influence. You want to fill their malleable little brains with more compelling subject matter. Something that will stretch their horizons and teach them about the world's complexities.

You push the pause button on the video recorder and say to them: "You don't really want to watch a movie you've already seen fifteen times, do you?" Your nieces look at you as if you've just revealed Santa Claus has cancer. "I mean, wouldn't you rather watch a documentary about young female warriors? Or the migratory patterns of birds?"

They continue to stare.

"I'm serious," you say. "Look, we could start with this video about surviving an avalanche."

They return their attention to the frozen image on the screen. "TURN IT BACK ON!" they shout. "Look! There's Nala! She and Simba are going to fall in love!"

THE SPOUSE

Now that you've eliminated parents, couples, and children from the approved list of viewing partners, all that remains is the spouse.

You know what kind of movies the spouse likes. The spouse knows what kind of movies you like. Over the years, you've managed to find five, maybe even six whole movies you've both liked equally well. Actually, that's not true. You only pretended to like *Titanic* because you went with a group and everyone else said they liked it.

Regardless, you approach the spouse one night over dinner.

"Honey. How about we rent a video tonight?" You keep your

voice light and a little high, the way you do when you desperately want something but don't want to appear as if you do.

"Tonight?" the spouse replies. "Are you *crazy?* It's the championship playoff game between the Boston Boweevils and the Dakota Tube Socks. It's the last game before the star player, Dikembe Idnani Garcia Chante Ramirez, is deported. There is no way I'm missing the game. Everyone has been talking about it. *Everyone.*"

ALONE

And so, in the end, you head to the video store alone. Ahhhh… a night to yourself. A night to choose whatever movie you want and watch it, without fear or compromise, in the comfort of your own living room.

You enter the store and head to the wall of new releases. But after a few minutes, you find you're not reading the titles because it's dawned on you that if you're going to rent something only you want to watch, something only you will appreciate, that maybe you should rent one of your favorite movies of all time. Something like *My Fair Lady* or *Funny Girl.* You like stories where flat-chested women surprise everyone. That settles it. *Funny Girl* it is.

Back at home, you pop the silver video disc into the player. The image starts skipping and little digitized boxes of color come and go in a senseless procession. The audio track is also scritching from one unrelated bit of dialogue to another. You remove the scratched disk, clean it, and put it back in. The movie is still unwatchable and you wonder why it is that *Funny Girl* attracts the kind of viewers who don't know the proper handling of a videodisc. And what this might, incidentally, say about you. You remove the disc, place it back into its plastic sleeve and turn off the video player.

Having exhausted all your video viewing options, you decide to grab a book, get into your favorite pajamas, climb into bed…and read. The second your eyes hit the page, you're happy. Absorbed. Complete. And it occurs to you that reading is perhaps what you should have been doing all along.

Time Sharing

Last spring, I spent four brutal months chasing after impossible deadlines, wailing and complaining the whole time like Lucy Ricardo after yet another fight with Ricky. At the time, Angela was juggling several complicated lawsuits and was unable to provide much in the way of comfort or diversion. In fact, for weeks on end, all we did was work, talk about work, and wish through clenched teeth that each other would just shut up about work for a change.

Sometime around April, we realized this was perhaps not the best way to manage a relationship. So we got out our date books, found four open days we shared, and booked a vacation at a hammock-and-pool resort south of Cancun, Mexico.

Now, let me state right up front I'm not the beach-vacation type. I burn in the sun. I'm self-conscious in a bathing suit. And, well, what is there to do on a beach anyway? My mind is the type that if not completely engaged, it will turn on me like a feral child, a situation I mostly like to avoid.

But at this particular resort, Angela assured me, I could hike and kayak and tour Mayan ruins. I wouldn't even have to look at the beach if I didn't want to. I could be busy as a leaf-cutter ant...or not. "You know, we could use the downtime," she said. She was right. We needed the time together.

After a three-and-a-half hour flight from Denver, we settled into our ocean-view room, went to dinner at a candle-lit open-air restaurant on the beach, ordered champagne, and promptly got into a huge, highly unattractivefight. I'll spare you the ghastly details, but our conversation started with the words

"You don't know what you're talking about," and progressed steadily downhill.

At first, I thought this would be one of those cathartic, air-your-grievances talks that all couples have now and then. I'd smile at the waiter when he'd come to refill our champagne glasses, and flash him one of those conspiratorial you-know-how-it-is looks. But as our conversation disintegrated, my smile faded, and I came to view both the waiter and Angela as arch enemies. The fight culminated when I sent the waiter and his bottle of champagne away.

"We don't need any more," I said. Angela called him back with the words: "Yes we do."

So I got up and started to march aggressively back to our room. It was a warm evening, with an almost-full moon reflecting on the black surface of the ocean. My hair whipped my face in the breeze. I huffed deep breaths of righteous indignation, as if playing a role in a movie-of-the-week drama. As I walked along the well-groomed walkway, I could hear Angela's sandals slapping the pavement behind me.

We arrived back at the room, slammed around the bathroom getting ready for bed, clicked off the lights, and proceeded to try and sleep. Angela clung to her side of the king-sized mattress; I gripped my own. Two purebred Newfoundlands could have lounged in the space between us.

During the night, I planned grand, daring escapes. I would wake early, pack my suitcase and tiptoe out the door. That would teach *her* not to fight with *me* on vacation. The note I'd leave would read simply: "See you in Denver." At two a.m., leaving Angela to enjoy the beach in Mexico seemed like the perfect punishment. Upon reconsideration, the strategy seems a little weak.

Since we weren't speaking, I'm not sure what thoughts Angela was harboring, but there was an awful lot of flipping and sighing and pillow pounding coming from her side of the bed, all of which filled me with a great deal of satisfaction.

At nine a.m., we ended the charade of sleep, and got up, rumpled and ragged. The morning sun was sparkling on the ocean. We could hear the gentle lapping of the surf. The orange flowers on our patio had opened in the daylight, emitting a light, sweet scent.

Shit.

It was a perfect day.

Worse yet, at check-in the day before, I'd signed us up for an orientation about a "membership program" that the concierge assured us would only take ninety minutes. For our time, we'd get a gift certificate to use for massages at the spa. I didn't care about the membership. I did, however, care about a massage.

"I'm not going," Angela said.

"Then don't," I replied, while intently applying mascara in the bathroom mirror.

"I won't. Unless you want me to."

"It's entirely up to you."

Both of us were clearly waiting for the other to give, just a little.

"You know," Angela said, "they're gonna try to get us to buy a time share or something."

"I know. But I want a tour of this place. And I'd like a free massage."

"Well…" she said, softening just a bit. "I wouldn't *mind* a tour."

I turned and looked her in the eyes for the first time in thirteen hours. I am childish and pouty and routinely make it a point not to be the first one to soften after a fight. But I also positively hate it when Angela is the first to show a little tenderness, primarily because it shows just how childish and pouty I really am.

"Okay, then," I said. "Why don't you come along?"

She got dressed and we walked together to the orientation. Halfway there, Angela mumbled an apology and I mumbled one back. It wasn't much. But it was a start.

• • •

The orientation took place in a small round meeting room next to a bar on the far side of the resort. The room had a thatched roof and yellow walls covered with large colorful posters advertising cruises and resorts and condominiums. There were several small tables around the room. At each one, a couple sat listening, their expressions non-committal, to a sales person in bright tropical clothing.

I instantly regretted bringing us here. As Angela had predicted, we were obviously in line for a time-share sales pitch, which was, like, so not us. We are people who routinely plunk ourselves down in the middle of foreign cities without much in the way of a budget or itinerary. We like not knowing where we're going to stay or eat or how much it's going to cost. It makes opening the credit card bill that much more thrilling.

Timeshares, on the other hand, are for people who like order and predictability. They're for people who eat at the same restaurants, order the same meals, and have freezers full of those miniature quiche appetizers from Costco. If we agreed to a time share, of all things, pretty soon we'd be signing up for bridge cruises and wearing t-shirts that proclaim: "I'm with stupid." The slope is just that slippery. Besides, this was a beach resort. Beach as in sunburn. Beach as in boring.

I turned to Angela. "Sorry for getting us into this."

"That's okay," she said. "I think we just make a pact that we're not going to buy anything."

I was tired, and still a bit miffed about the fight, but not so tired and miffed that I didn't like the notion of a pact. "Fine by me," I said.

Within minutes, we were seated in front of a deeply tanned woman named Janet who had thin gold rings on every finger. She began asking us questions, using the italicized cadence of a kindergarten teacher.

"So," she said, "How important are vacations to the two of you?"

"Vacations are very important," Angela replied.

Janet turned her gaze to me. "Is that *true?*"

"Yep."

I glanced at Angela and her dark brown eyes smiled at mine.

Janet continued. "And if the two of you could travel *more* often for *less* money, would you *like* that?"

"Sure," I said.

And thus our conversation progressed. In our weakened post-combat state, Janet skillfully managed to get us to admit that vacations were important, that we spent a lot of money on them, that perhaps we didn't always get the best value for our money, and that yeah, sure, we *would* like to hear about their fantastic, one-of-a-kind travel membership club.

"Great!" Janet replied. "And remember, this is not a time-share. It's a money-saving *opportunity.*"

Angela and I shared another subtle-but-knowing glance. Uniting against Janet and the Vast North Atlantic Time-Share Conspiracy was turning out to be the perfect reconciliatory exercise. I settled back into my chair, confident that no matter what Janet promised, Angela and I would walk out of there together without giving her a dime of satisfaction.

Oblivious to our pact, Janet proceeded to explain the myriad money-saving benefits of the membership. She spoke earnestly of travel agency discounts, condominium networks and rock-bottom cruise prices. I listened without hearing. I simply watched Janet's mouth move as if it were somehow disconnected from her face, as if it were a set of wind-up teeth chattering in the air between us. The ceiling fan created a slight breeze against my bare arms. A blender whirred in the distance. Some time later, Janet completed her list of benefits and drew us back into the conversation.

"So, what do you two do for a living?" she asked.

I said I was a writer.

"Ohhh, I *love* to read," Janet replied. "I just loved *The DaVinci Code.*"

She then turned to Angela.

"And you?"

"I'm a lawyer."

Janet sat up straight, suddenly very interested. She asked Angela what kind of law she practiced, what cases she was working on, and—hey!—would she like a margarita? "You just sit right there. I'll get it for you."

As Janet strode toward the bar to get us some wallet-opening cocktails, I turned to Angela. "Now the pressure's really going to increase."

"I know," she replied. "But I like Janet. And you know, the program sounds kind of interesting."

I wasn't sure I heard correctly. "What did you say?"

"I said the program sounds interesting."

Suddenly, and without any advance notice, our thinly constructed pact was in danger of collapse.

• • •

Janet returned with our drinks and proceeded to take us on a tour of the resort. She led us along flowered walkways to several blue-green swimming pools. We toured the spa, which smelled like lavender. We wandered in and out of restaurants with marble floors and indoor waterfalls. The resort was lovely, and I would have said so, but Angela had begun to ask a worrisome list of questions about the membership package. One of us had to be strong.

I fell behind and began to perfect my polite-but-disinterested look. Why I had to work on it I'm not sure, since this is the look I walk around with most often.

Ahead of me, I could hear Janet talking to Angela about the high-end lodging units known as *casitas* that were reserved solely for members. "Would you like to *see* a *casita?*" she asked, while leading us up the walkway toward one.

She unlocked the door and led us into a large welcoming room with a thatched roof, private patio and unobstructed view of the Mexican Caribbean, which was just steps away. The king-sized bed was draped in soft mosquito netting, and on it sat a swan artfully constructed from rolled white towels. The swan was surrounded by a sprinkling of fresh red rose petals.

I found the swan to be a little cheesy, and felt the rose petals definitely belonged in the overdoing-it category. Angela, on the other hand, was enchanted. The last of her pre-arranged reticence crumbled, and she began twirling from one end of the tiled room to the other. "Look! A hot tub! Look! A private toilet! Look! Two Sinks!"

Angela, it must be said, is frequently delighted by small things. She adores the hot towels given to us when we arrive at our local sushi restaurant. She loves the button on her watch that makes it glow green. And the cardboard box of snack items handed out on airplanes is enough to keep her humming happily for well over an hour.

Two sinks and a toweled swan? We were doomed.

As Angela turned the bathroom faucets on and off, Janet continued to recite the membership benefits, and I stepped up my resistance efforts.

"So," Janet said, turning her attention toward me. "Do you like *cruises?*"

"No. Not really."

"Do you work with a *travel* agent?"

"Never."

"Do you stay at many *condominiums?*"

"Not if we can help it."

We left the casita and I walked along, relishing the small bit of power I'd acquired.

• • •

Upon arriving back at the sales room, Janet began to calculate the endless number of ways we would be able to save money with the resort's not-a-time-share program. She made her calculations upside down, so that we could see them from across the table. This impressed me greatly, and instead of focusing on the numbers themselves and what they meant, I became transfixed by Janet's ability to write an upside-down five. This soon led to thoughts about how many times she had made these calculations for other gullible vacationers, and how it was, exactly, that Angela had become so easily ensnared.

Mostly, though, I wondered how much longer this would continue. We'd been at it for three hours already, and were still, best I could tell, a considerable distance away from that massage certificate. I could only hope that despite Angela's interest, our pact would hold.

Another hour passed. A manager was called. Binders were consulted. More perks were added. And finally, the actual price of the not-a-time-share was given to us. Angela and I went to lunch to talk it over.

• • •

We sat down in an outdoor restaurant next to one of the swimming pools. Nearby, a young, sunburned couple sat eating cheeseburgers in their bathing suits. I braced myself.

"Well?" I asked.

"I'm completely sold on this," Angela said.

It was worse than I'd anticipated. Interested was one thing. Completely sold was another.

"I'm serious," Angela said. "I think this is perfect for us."

We ordered lunch and she spent the next fifteen minutes explaining why this vacation arrangement was perfect for our lifestyle. I didn't want to listen. What I wanted to do was cover my ears with my hands and start singing something obnoxious. Something like *La Cucaracha*. Given our recent fight, this didn't seem particularly well advised. So I strived to pay attention.

And then it was my turn. I calmly explained how nothing Janet had promised was actually written into the contract. How, without written reassurances, we could lose a lot of money. It was a good argument. Rational. Clear-headed. I impressed even myself. Angela listened without speaking, her chin resting on her fist. And when I finished, she agreed. "You're right," she said.

"I'm right?" Although I knew it would be tough for Angela to argue with a contract deficiency, I still wasn't sure she'd want to give up on that swan so easily.

"Yes," she said. "Nothing they promised has been written down."

Damn.

Once again, Angela was the first to relax her stance. I had no choice but to try and reciprocate. I picked up my water glass, which was dripping wet from the humidity, and took a swallow. "What if they could prove the benefits are real," I asked, setting the glass back down. "Do you really want to do this?"

We began talking about the not-a-time-share package and what it really offered us. And as we talked, I thought about how much I've always appreciated our ability to have well-reasoned conversations like this—that is, when we're not fighting. Over the course of ten years, we've bought and sold homes, seen each other through career changes, and endured family feuds, the loss of loved ones, and one fairly grueling kitchen remodeling. Always, our ability to talk has sustained us. Wasn't a lack of conversation what caused us to take this vacation in the first place—what caused our misunderstanding the previous night?

The waiter cleared our dishes and we continued to converse, rationally, like well-adjusted adults, for over an hour. I was still skeptical and hugely reluctant to purchase the membership primarily because nowhere on my list of goals have the words "time share" ever appeared. If I crossed over to the beach-going mainstream, could I still listen to National Public Radio and attend poetry slams? Not that I've ever actually attended a poetry slam, but I'd like to think I'd be welcome at one.

Then Angela brought up a point that lasered through my defenses.

"If nothing else," she said, "a membership like this would force us to schedule more time away together."

I looked at her face, and then at her dark curls—curls that spring crazily from her head in damp tropical climates. How could I not want to spend more time with someone who has such happy vacation hair? So I agreed to pursue the membership, but only if Janet could put her promises in writing.

Back at the sales room, we explained our concerns to Janet, who promptly provided reams of written reassurance. Within no time, Angela and I were signing our names to a stack of documents granting us one hundred weeks of not-a-time-share happiness. As a special thank-you, Janet also upgraded us to the casita with the swan and two sinks.

• • •

The next morning, after collecting our massages at the spa, Angela and I strolled down to the beach. She reclined in the sun, while I sat under a palapa smoothing on a one-eighth inch layer of SPF 45 sunblock. Angela called to me from her lounge chair. "What do you want to do this afternoon?"

I answered honestly: "Absolutely nothing." Four months of deadlines, one night of fighting, and eight hours of time-share negotiations had taken their toll. I was finally ready to embrace the benefits of beach vacations.

For three days, I lay in a hammock, read books and stared at the ocean. I didn't swim, kayak, hike, shop, find a museum, or take a Spanish class. I did, however, obsess about becoming a member of the time-share community. But only slightly. And when I wasn't reading, or napping, or wondering what kind of person I'd become, I was talking over long meals with Angela about how I may not always know what's best for me, but that I'm glad we know what's best for us.

Even if it takes us a while to get there.

In Praise of Reunions

I have just a few minutes to talk here. Just a few, precious, solitary minutes before I must head to the airport and pick up my three sisters—two from California, one from Kansas—for our bi-annual sister reunion, our once-every-two-years' chance to push life aside and get caught up with one another.

Now, I'm not sure if you have sisters or not. If not, you may picture my impending reunion and envision four young girls in pastel dresses combing each other's hair and sharing the yellow marshmallow chicks from their Easter baskets. That's certainly one possible scenario.

But if you do have sisters, and if you've attempted reunions with them after growing up and becoming the lone sushi-eating Democrat amongst a trio of pot roast Republicans; and if you've ever had reunions and felt that somehow, even though you share the same gene pool, there must have been a glitch in the genetic coding because, really, these people couldn't possibly be related to you; and, if you've had these thoughts and immediately felt yourself weighted down by a leaded X-ray blanket of guilt for even thinking not-so-nice things about your sisters, well, then, thanks. I accept your sympathy.

Don't get me wrong. I love my sisters, and feel firmly anchored in the world because of them. After all, no one but a sister can remind you of the full jagged range of emotions you possess—from love to envy to irritation—all in the efficient space of one telephone call. It's just that family reunions, like holidays and weddings, are fraught with what you might call "issues."

I'm third out of four girls, and at various points in our small, tract-house upbringing, I have been the youngest, the middle child, and the eldest daughter, so I'm not sure how birth order may influence how I feel about reunions. I only know that in the past, I've been a teensy bit uptight about them. And, well, let's just say my therapist is grateful she was an only child.

But I'm older now. And far more secure in who I am. I no longer feel that Debbie is more fashionable, Pam more intelligent, and Tami just plain luckier and more blessed than all of us combined. Plus, she has a killer figure. But that no longer bothers me. Really.

You see, after several reunions at various points in our adult lives, reunions that occurred with new babies, after divorces, and featured a hideous parade of hairstyles, I can honestly say I am more comfortable and at peace with who I am.

(Editor's Note: In the past week, Shari has gotten her hair cut and colored, endured a facial waxing, and spent hours at the mall selecting two new outfits, only one of which was on sale. She also embarked on a daily running program, somehow believing she could lose two years' worth of overindulgence in five, short-but-determined days.)

Because I'm more content with my life, I've chosen not to plan a full schedule of activities for the reunion. Instead, I'm perfectly happy to just relax with my sisters in my humble Denver abode.

(Shari spent the last two weekends redecorating a guest bedroom. She bought a new comforter, end tables, lamps, and artwork. She bought four bouquets of flowers, scrubbed the fish tank twice, and spent a good thirty minutes choosing the most pleasing-but-unobtrusive scents for the plug-in air fresheners. "Fresh Linen" and "Juicy Pear" won out.)

In the past, when I used to be insecure about such matters, I would spend a week making cookies, appetizers, and desserts, and an entire evening pre-setting the dining room table with seasonally appropriate colors and accessories. Today, I'm pleased to report, the table is not yet set, and I won't even *start* making dinner until my sisters arrive. I've come that far. Besides, we're only having steaks and salad.

(Yes...but. Shari drove across town to buy prime-aged beef tenderloins from a specialty meat shop. She invested in French vinegar and olive oil for the salad. She looked through approximately forty-three cookbooks in search of the perfect, nothing-to-it last minute dessert, ultimately choosing grilled pears with raspberry coulis. She also made two liquor store runs in order have on hand every possible combination of alcohol for every possible drink that might be requested, including, but not limited to: Cosmopolitans, Bloody Marys, White Russians, Brandy Alexanders, and Screwdrivers. She also purchased red wine, white wine, dry champagne, sweet champagne, and beer. Oddly, two of her sisters don't even drink.)

After spending our first night together enjoying a mature, laid-back meal at home, I thought it would be nice—on the first full day of our reunion—to take a drive into the mountains and stop for a massage.

(At one of the best spas in Colorado.)

Then, after our day at the spa, we could go downtown for a nice dinner somewhere to celebrate Debbie's birthday.

(Somewhere? Let's just say that the restaurant was pre-selected after consulting two restaurant guides, an online dining site, and one well-connected, in-the-know hairdresser.)

And that's it. That's the extent of my planning. Gone are the days when I would nervously cram our schedule with movies, classes, shopping, photo shoots, and other activities that would allow us to maintain the illusion of sisterly togetherness without actually having to converse with one another.

This year, by gum, I'm confident in our ability—or perhaps it's just *my* ability—to sit back and see what unfolds. Perhaps we'll rehash childhood stories. Perhaps we'll dissect our adult relationships. Perhaps we'll talk about menopause, although I'd really prefer not to.

Well, I really must be going now. I don't want to be late for their flights. I'm feeling so at ease and comfortable with myself that I really can't wait to be with my sis…

Oh, shoot.

Wait just a minute while I straighten the photos on the piano.

There. That's better.

Like I was saying. It's taken a while but I've finally realized that my three sisters are people with whom I've not only had the longest relationships of my life, they are also the only people on earth with whom I can truly relax and be myself.

Yes, it's taken a lot of work to get to this newly secure and confident place. And perhaps that's the real point of family reunions. They're not just about catching up with your sisters. They're also about catching up with yourself.

THE REAL DIGITAL DIVIDE

Two months ago, I decided to create a website. I made this decision with the same breezy indifference I use in selecting my morning coffee cup, as in: Today, I'll use the blue mug I bought in Mendocino. Next Tuesday, I'll create a website. Simple, right?

Actually, it was fairly simple—when I was working alone to gather the material for the site. But once I hired a web designer, things grew to a staggering level of complexity. For the sake of this story, let's call the web designer Like Totally, for that seemed to be one of his favorite expressions.

About two weeks into the process, Like Totally called to tell me a draft of my site was on the web. I logged on, began to navigate my way through the site, and quickly discovered that whenever I clicked onto a new page I could not click back to where I began. I called the web designer.

"The site looks great," I explained. "But when I reach certain pages I can't go back."

"Go back?" he asked, plainly mystified by my question. "Like, why would you want to do that? All you have to do is close out the page."

"Close out?" I didn't know what he was talking about.

"Yes, just close out the page and you'll get where you were previously."

"But I never navigate the web that way," I protested. "Closing out is far too risky. What if I can't get back where I started?"

Mr. Totally started to chuckle. "Wow," he said. "You must

be naïve and unsophisticated and like totally inept at web navigation. *Go back?*" His laughter intensified and I could hear him slapping the armrest of his chair.

Over the next few days, I conducted an informal poll among friends and discovered that the world does indeed consist of two kinds of people: go-backs and close-outs. It was information I could not readily accept. For me, hitting the back button is such a natural, no-brainer way to traverse the Internet that I couldn't believe there might be other, equally effective ways to move around in cyberspace.

But as I thought about it, I realized web navigation is something most of us teach ourselves based on some intuitive sense of order and direction. That being the case, I began to wonder what a person's navigational preference might say about his or her personality.

Go-backs, it seemed to me, would be people who like having links to the past and probably have many long-term friendships. Go-backs are probably impulsive web users, the kind of people who start out looking for research on the consumer confidence index and end up on a site about the Whirling Dervishes of southern Turkey who, incidentally, only whirl once a year. Because go-backs are also insecure about technology—and their enormous capacity for distraction—they need a digital handrail to guide them back to where they started. In the world of the Internet, go-backs are the impetuous kindergartners who climb the schoolyard fence, get caught, and then beg for a second chance. Go backs are my people.

Now, let's talk about close-outs. People who shut down web pages when done with them are clearly more decisive and confident than go-backs, and they're probably not given to fond recollections. They're forward thinkers who gather data, make decisions and emphatically stand by them. They don't dawdle, which makes them reliable, but they may have a tendency to be a bit brash. Close-outs scare me.

In conducting my poll, I was pleased to discover that the people I work best with are just like me. They like to go back.

Like Dorothy from *The Wizard of Oz*, we believe there's no place like home.

I was, however, astonished to learn that my beloved is a close-out, which actually helps to explain some of our arguments. "Honey, let's go back to when you first got upset," I might say. "No!" she'll reply. "It's over. I'm not talking about this any more."

Now, I've taken just about every personality assessment known to humankind. The Myers-Briggs tells me I'm introspective, intuitive, feeling, and perceptive. The Strong Interest Inventory reveals that I'm artistic, social, and enterprising. In astrology, I'm a Taurus. In Numerology, a five. Furthermore, I fully understand people can have vastly different viewpoints based on gender, skin color, sexual orientation, religion, income, and whether they read *Tattoo Magazine* or *The Economist*. Still, I was completely dumbstruck to learn that people also differ in how they navigate the web. Do the differences never end?

Then it hit me that all the assessments, valuations, and tests that promise to reveal our true personality type and how to use that knowledge to relate to others are all saying the same thing: We're different, so get over it. No, no—that's not what they're saying. What they're saying is that the best way to get along with others is to understand how we're different.

Well, that's great. In theory. But the fact is there are so many potential areas of difference between people that it often doesn't even occur to us that a difference might exist. Maybe, in addition to trying to understand and embrace the big distinctions—i.e., introvert versus extrovert, young versus old, black versus white—it might make sense to be alert for the small differences as well. "You check your e-mail at the *end* of the day? Tell me more."

Unfortunately when it came to my website, Like Totally was not able to accommodate both close-outs and go-backs. The difficulty had something to do with browser liposuction and HTML backsplash or some such thing. However, knowing there are different ways of navigating the web, I researched what worked best for my particular audience and designed the site accordingly.

As you might expect, every page on my site is now accompanied by a soothing little back button that helps users find their place in the world.

Beat It

Recently, I was invited to a party thrown in celebration of the eighties, the Ronald Reagan-Pac Man-Ghostbusters decade. The party invitation was explicit in its instructions: You *must* (bold-faced and color-coded) dress in eighties attire.

Groan.

I hate parties that come with instructions. Aren't parties strenuous enough without having to worry about being socially ostracized for failing to dress as the host requests?

Truth be told, social ostracism was not the real reason I didn't want to dress up in eighties attire. I didn't want to dress up because I didn't know what combination of clothing would best represent the person I was back then. Should I wear aviator glasses, denim overalls and flat leather sandals like the hippie college student I embodied during the first part of the eighties? Or should I dress in a blue suit and floppy white bow tie like the dress-for-success career woman I professed to be my first year out of college? Or should I wear dirty blue jeans like the European backpacker I became when I came to the belated-but-fortunate realization that bow ties were not my style?

Not sure what version of my younger self to present, I chose to dress like Michael Jackson. Not the white-washed, red-lipped, reassembled-all-wrong puzzle piece that he is today. But rather, Michael Jackson, circa 1982. The *Beat It* Michael Jackson. The white-gloved Michael Jackson. The King of Pop with tight black pants, gold-rim dark glasses and stratospheric record sales. For added authenticity, I got ahold of a stuffed monkey and called it Bubbles.

Now, normally costume parties fill me with stomach-flipping dread. I fear I'm going to look dumb. That I'll spend all this time on a costume and no one will notice. That I will spend all this time on a costume and *everyone* will notice. But when I put on the curly black wig, wriggled my left hand into a white glove, and picked up my monkey, I felt proudly transformed. Dressed like Michael Jackson, I would stand out from the crowd, certainly. But I could also hide behind dark glasses and hope that people would find me too creepy to actually converse with. How perfect.

So I arrive at the party pleased with my attention-getting-yet-repellingly-weird costume and spot one of my very best friends who's also dressed like—who else?—Michael Jackson. She's dressed like Michael Jackson, circa 1989: smooth hair, black glasses, and a luxurious red and gold leather jacket that resembles a royal uniform. Damn. She looks better than me.

So here we are: two Michaels surrounded by several other manifestations of eighties American style. There is a hard rocker with leather fringe jacket and ripped blue jeans. There are several women wearing tight leggings and lace-up Reebok tennis shoes, looking as if they've just arrived from an advanced Jazzercise class. Another woman is dressed like Sue Ellen from Dallas, all moussed hair, chunky earrings, and linebacker shoulder pads.

The party begins, the music grows louder, and the sound of record albums we haven't heard for twenty years hurtle us back in time. We wax nostalgic about our lives two decades earlier when we were: students, married, poor, stoned…or all of the above. We paste photos of our younger selves on a white board labeled, *The Wall of Shame.* After tacking my photo to the wall, I stand back astonished to realize that with my aviator glasses and curly permed hair, I actually *did* look like Michael Jackson back then.

But at some point, I'm not sure when, I begin to realize I am no longer remotely like my younger curly-haired self.

It could be while trying to fake lip-synch my way through the lyrics of a Men At Work song I've long since forgotten. Or when I decline a beer and then a sandwich and then a slice of cake because, well, there's this diet I'm on. Perhaps it's when I realize I cannot have a third glass of wine because, if you must know, I now find it difficult to sleep when I drink.

Actually, I think the moment of reckoning occurs the moment I start dancing. What can I say? The group wants the two Michaels to dance. I'll spare you the despicable details, but two white women well into their forties cannot break-dance with the crisp, exhilarating choreography of Jacko. We do, however, try.

We thrust our limbs outward in spastic blasts, looking not cool but rather like we've been shot through with electricity. We spin around and around and around, stopping dizzily in front of a vacant hallway as opposed to the living room audience we are aiming for. Plus, we get winded. No, that's understating it. In reality, we find ourselves buckled over and gasping like we've been chasing a bus down the highway. About the only bona fide Michael maneuver we can perform involves cupping our crotches with our hands. I don't sense onlookers are terribly disappointed when we stop.

We hobble off into a nearby bathroom to cool down. The other Michael peels off her sticky leather jacket. I wriggle out from under the curly black wig, look at my sweaty, smashed hair, and began to tally up the results of the evening.

One. I've had to watch what I eat.

Two. I've had to watch what I drink.

Three, four, and five: I've suffered from memory failure, overexertion, and the mind-bending realization that I actually spent four hours this afternoon looking for a black fedora so that I could look like Michael Jackson.

What a party.

And so, at about 10:30, when the conversation is slowing and the games are over, I follow the other Michael out the door and beat it home. On the way, it dawns on me that I took more time preparing for the party than actually being at the party. In the real eighties, parties burst spontaneously from the landscape and lasted six, eight, ten hours without any preparation at all. How exhausting.

I arrive home at eleven o'clock, remove my white glove, make a cup of tea and snuggle into flannel pajamas. Within ten minutes, I'm inside warm soft sheets reveling in the supreme happiness that comes from getting home—sober—at a decent hour, and without the sound of loud music ringing in my eardrums.

Avoiding a Hostel Takeover

Next week, I will be attending a conference in the Rocky Mountains where the youth-hostel accommodations consist of a room with two sets of wooden bunk beds, a sway-back queen mattress, an enormous table lamp straight off the set of a seventies sitcom, and a view into the men's public restroom, which is not as interesting as you might imagine. Total cost of lodging? Twenty dollars per night, plus an additional three dollars for guests who fail to bring their own sheets and towels.

I speak with authority about the lodging because I attended the same conference last year and somehow managed to convince myself—in between searching for ear plugs and waiting for the Germans to get out of the shower—that even though I'm over forty, youth hostels were still "pretty neat." Truth be known, the only reason I could endure the accommodations was because I managed to snag a room all to myself.

I signed up for the conference this year after being assured I could again have a private room. Knowing I could escape to the seclusion of my own digs made it easier to accept spending five days attending breakfast, lunch, dinner, all workshops, and the bathroom with the other attendees.

But about a month ago, my private haven became threatened when the conference organizer told me I was one of only two people out of twenty-eight to be granted a private room. "Only two of you are snobby and anti-social enough to hog whole rooms to yourselves," she said. Actually, she didn't say that. But that's how I interpreted her comment.

I imagined arriving at breakfast well rested from a night of solitary slumber only to hear others complain about room-mates who snore, sleepwalk, talk aloud, and read until two in the morning. *"What?"* they would ask upon learning I didn't have a roommate. "What makes *you* special?" Despite these misgivings, I reasoned it was better to feel like a prima donna than to negotiate with strangers over who gets the bottom bunk.

Then, three days ago, the situation got even worse when the conference organizer happened to mention there were now several people on the waiting list. "You snotty, so-above-it-all Queen Bee. If you didn't have to have your own room, then everybody who wished to attend the conference could do so," she said.

Actually, she didn't say that. But regardless of what she said—or meant, I began to descend into an ugly pit of self-loathing. I started to feel that wanting to change my clothes in private was immature, that the desire for a good night's sleep was selfish. I was ashamed I made enough money to afford to the extra fifty dollars it took to secure a private room for five nights. What was wrong with me anyway?

As the self-loathing exhausted itself, the cavalry of anger intervened. I grew resentful. How *dare* they hint that I should give up my room? Private rooms were offered as an option. They should have planned better. It wasn't my responsibility to accommodate *their* lack of foresight.

Unfortunately, the anger was short-lived for paranoia soon took charge. I managed to convince myself that the other attendees were part of a secret youth hostel society happily traveling the globe, trying on each other's pajamas, and talking with great eye-rolling disdain about people who couldn't share their space. Sure, other conference goers had told me they too were worried about the accommodations. But I assumed they said these things to publicly throw me off-guard, while pri-vately they passed notes about my pimply-faced modesty. Why couldn't I be like everyone else?

Then, from a foggy distance, I heard my mother's voice: "Shari, would you leap off the Golden Gate Bridge simply because everyone else did?" She used to trot out this line whenever I tried to convince her I needed a certain type of shoes because all my friends wore them. Although the analogy didn't work when I was a teenager, something about it made me wise up where the youth hostel was concerned.

Reason began to take hold, and I listed my rationale for wanting a private room: One: I never liked slumber parties as a kid; Two: As someone who works from home, I'm not used to sharing space with people; and, Three: Even when I was twenty-four and touring Europe on twenty dollars a day, I managed to avoid youth hostels. I'm just not a group-going gal.

Realizing this, I gave up the idea of staying at the hostel altogether and rented a small cabin on a lake just minutes from the conference location. Next week, I'll still be able to eat and interact with the other participants by day, but at night I'll be able to unwind—and shower—in my own private nirvana.

This has several advantages, as you might expect. One: I get my own space. Two: I don't have to bring my own sheets. Three: I'm now looking forward to the conference. And four: there is now room at the hostel for more people to attend.

Armed with my own private cabin, I'm now feeling so good about next week's conference that I'm actually eager to interact with others. I'm even thinking that maybe, just maybe, I'll invite a few folks over for a pajama party.

TEACHING LESSONS

When I was in college, I imagined myself returning to the classroom one day, not as a flailing, floundering student, but as a calm, learned professor. A professor who was wise, but jovial. Stern, but inspirational. The kind of professor whose magnetic presence guided students, like a mariner's compass, toward their successful destinies.

I imagined a future student writing me at the end of the semester:

Professor Caudron,

You helped me realize my true calling is not to be a beautician after all. I now want to be a brain surgeon. For this, I am 4-ever grateful. Sincerely, Tiffany.

As the years passed, the teaching dream intensified. I'd crafted a modestly successful writing career. I'd written about business, law, medicine, popular culture, travel, and science. I'd acquired the temerity to use the word *temerity* in sentences. Clearly, today's students needed my special brand of insight.

And so, recently, I accepted my first teaching position. The assignment? Teaching English composition to a class of twenty-five community college students ranging in age from seventeen to fifty.

WEEK ONE

Our class meets once a week at six p.m. in a bright new classroom with computers at every desk. On the first night of class, the students arrive and sit quietly upright, their new textbooks

145

stacked neatly in front of them. To break the silence, I ask them to share their feelings about writing research papers.

"It keeps you open minded," says a young woman with long brown hair.

"You learn new stuff," says a young man with a ring in his tongue. The ring clicks softly against his teeth.

A sandy-haired student named Lennie raises his hand.

"Yes, Lennie?"

"I think writing papers is hard, but you learn a lot and it is always worth it at the end," he says.

"Thank you, Lennie," I say. Lennie smiles and clasps his hands in front of him.

I tell students they've done a good job impressing me, but now I'd like to know what they really think about writing. The students look at each other like I'm asking which one broke the window with a baseball.

"Confusing?" one student says, as if she is asking a question.

"Painful?" suggests another.

I turn and write their words on the whiteboard with a blue marker. This encourages them and soon they are hurtling opinions faster than I can record them.

"Writing is like getting your teeth pulled."

"It's like digging a hole and you don't know how deep to go."

"It's like opening the washing machine after wet clothes have been sitting there moldering in the dark for several days."

Very impressive, I think to myself. He used the word moldering.

Week Two

We talk about the first assignment, which is to observe a subculture and write about it. I tell students I not only want to know what members of the subculture look and sound like, but I also want to know what conclusions they can make about the subculture based on their observations. Hands raise.

"What's a subculture?"

I explain: doll collectors, Star Trek fans, people who believe in the presence of aliens. It's any group that shares the same values, beliefs, and codes of conduct. More hands raise.

"Can I view people at a bar?" asks a woman with a black tattoo on her wrist.

"How about my family?" asks the student with the tongue ring. "They're kinda weird."

I explain that I'd like them to step outside their comfort zones and observe a subculture they're not familiar with.

"Miss Caudron?" asks a student with red hair braids. "I can't drive more than two miles from my house and there are no subcultures where I live."

On the break, one of the older students comes up to me and suggests that perhaps this might be a teensy bit difficult for the first assignment. "You know," she says, "for some of the younger students."

WEEK THREE

I grade the first set of papers; they are stacked on my desk in purple and lime green and yellow folders. Most of the students have managed to find a subculture to observe, and I'm impressed with the detail they've included about clothing and language. But reading the essays, I have no idea what their own impressions are. I communicate this to the class.

"Many of you failed to communicate your opinions of the subculture," I say. "I want to know your point of view. Your *thesis*."

"Thesis?" they say, looking at each other as if I've just acquired a lisp.

WEEK FIVE

Two weeks of backpedaling and students finally understand what a thesis is and why it's important. But I now face a new problem. We're starting to conduct more formal research, and I've asked them to find an authority on their subculture to interview.

Lennie raises his hand. "So, like, we're building on our knowledge about our subcultures, right?"

"Exactly," I say, relieved to have Lennie—instead of me—pointing out the logic in the assignment.

"That's cool," Lennie says. Lennie likes to please me. This is a quality I find highly admirable.

The student sitting directly behind Lennie speaks up. "When you say interview, do you mean call up somebody you don't know?"

"Sure," I say. "Someone who's an expert on the topic."

"Then what?"

"Then ask him or her questions."

"I can't just call someone I don't *know.*"

"Why not?" I ask, my voice brimming with teacherly encouragement. "I'm merely asking you to interview someone on the phone. I'm not asking you to have tea with a mass murderer." I chuckle, pleased by my cleverness.

The students stare at me.

After several long seconds, Cristina, the waitress in the back row, raises one pink hand in the air. "Ms. Caudron?" she says.

"Call me Shari," I say.

"Okay. Ms. Caudron, I don't know who to call."

I tell Cristina and the rest of the students if they are having trouble identifying an expert to see me on the break—which they do. She and several other students crowd around me like sheep and do their best to convince me there is absolutely no one available anywhere in the city-state-country-continent-planet-solar system-galaxy-universe with whom they can talk about their subjects.

I tell them to keep trying, that I'm sure they'll be successful.

WEEK SEVEN

They hate me. I can feel it. I've just handed back the second set of papers and they're upset I deducted points for such trivial matters as spelling, punctuation, and meeting the basic requirements of the assignment.

"You deducted five points for *that?*"

"We needed more *time.*"

"This class is too *hard.*"

But students are not only distressed by their grades, they also do not appear to be charmed by the friendly purple pen I used to correct their papers.

"Man...look at my paper!" says one of the more popular students. "It's like Barbie's been here."

I don't get this. The students are supposed to be respectful and enchanted by my experience. They're supposed to be appreciating all the hours/days/weekends I've invested in grading their papers and telling them what, exactly, didn't work and why. They're supposed to be learning from the comments I generously write in the margins of their papers. Comments such as:

Your thesis is unclear.

This is an incomplete sentence.

Quit *whining.*

Actually, I didn't write "quit whining" on their papers. It wouldn't even occur to me to do that.

Week Eight

I ask students to raise their hands if they find themselves getting confused during the research and writing process. Several hands go up.

"That's *perfect,*" I say. "That means you are real writers. Writing is about *thinking,* and if you're *thinking* it means you're trying to figure something out." I pause briefly to wonder why it is I'm now speaking in italics. Is this a *teacher* thing? I continue the lecture. "Like I was saying, when you're trying to figure something out, you're naturally going to be confused. In fact, you may have to write and revise several times before you understand what it is you're trying to accomplish."

The students gape at me with vacant faces. They do not find this insight reassuring. Even Lennie, who I've come to count on in such situations, remains silent.

WEEK NINE

I spend the entire weekend creating my lesson plan for the week. I write it. Revise it. Write it. Revise it. It's been like this every weekend since the semester started. I'm never quite sure if what I'm doing is the right thing or not, and I'm certain my inexperience shows. Five or six drafts later, I'm finally satisfied with my lesson plan.

WEEK TEN

I give students class time to start conducting research for their next paper. They start to work and I walk around class to see if anyone needs assistance.

The snowboarder in the beanie cap is sending an e-mail to a friend. Cristina can't find any information about her topic. "I *hate* my topic," she says. I overhear the student with the wrist tattoo whispering that she is sick of writing these damned papers.

And then I notice Keith, an athletic young man who never utters a word in class. He's already generated a lengthy list of potential sources.

And then I see Heather, dear Heather, who turns in flawless typewritten assignments and redid her first paper in order to raise her grade from ninety-six points to a perfect one hundred. Heather is working on an outline.

Next to her sits Dolores, who'd like to be a nurse someday. "I think back on the papers I used to write and I realize now how terrible they were," she says. "I'm getting a much better sense of what writing entails."

I look at Dolores and resist the urge to kiss her.

WEEK ELEVEN.

It's springtime now and the weather is warming up and even though ours is a night class, it's still light outside when class begins. The mood of students is shifting, growing lighter.

Week Twelve

Tonight, I've cancelled class in order to meet individually with each student. They come in, one by one, and we discuss the grades on their last assignment as well as their overall standing in the class.

I meet with Kathy, a young woman whose pastel underwear is frequently winking out from the top of her blue jeans. She's close to failing the course. "Do you have any questions about the upcoming paper or your grade thus far?" I ask.

"No. Not really. Can I go now?"

The meetings continue. Several people are pleasantly surprised by their grades. Three of four of them ask detailed questions about the final paper. Many of them find it weird to be chatting with the teacher.

After three hours of meetings, the last student arrives for her conference. Her name is Kaitlyn. She is an older woman who works hard but has found writing difficult. "You're very tolerant," she says. "People complain a lot in this class, but I think you're doing a good job. I'm learning a lot."

I smile at Kaitlyn thinking that if my heart wasn't already committed to Dolores, I'd propose to her on the spot.

Week Fourteen

Because we're nearing the end of the semester, I ask students to break into small groups and brainstorm about what they've learned about the writing process. When through, they make mini-presentations to the class.

"We overestimated our abilities," they say.

"The class was harder and took a lot more time than we thought."

"We got fixated on problems and wanted to quit."

Yeah, I'm thinking. Me too.

Callie, a bright young woman in her first year of college, walks to front of the class and I ask what advice she would give future students about how to succeed in the course. She picks up her necklace and chews on its gold chain. She thrusts her right hip to one side. "Um," she says. "I guess what I'd tell them is that even though the work is hard, they will learn a lot and they *will* get better if they stay with it."

Week Sixteen

The students turn in their final papers and we talk, conversationally, about the last four months of class. They ask me what secrets I've learned that enabled me to succeed as a professional writer. I tell them the only secret I know, and that I don't think it's much of a secret.

"You have to stick with it," I say. "Writing is not a linear process like everyone makes it out to be. You don't start out with 'In the beginning' and write perfect unedited prose until you type 'The end.' Actually, it's more like this."

I walk to the whiteboard and quickly draw a series of green overlapping circles.

"See, when you're learning something new, you move forward and then backward and then forward and then backward in wild looping spirals until eventually you generate enough forward momentum to complete a new project. Along the way, there will be setbacks. You'll doubt yourself. You'll get mad at others. You'll want to quit. But then, at some point, you'll find yourself celebrating some small success, and then another, and then another, until the project is complete and you realize you are capable of accomplishing more than you thought."

Lennie, who's decided he likes me again, raises his hand.

"Yes, Lennie?"

"You told us at the beginning of class that you'd been writing for, what was it, twenty years?"

"That's right."

"And you still go through this process everytime you start something new?"

The students look at me, waiting to see if I'll admit to feeling as confused and uncertain as they have the last few months.

"Yes, Lennie," I say, "I do go through this process whenever I do something new. And I'm surprised by the difficulty every single time."

SAWBONES

I was rushing through the white-tented terminal building at Denver International Airport when my attention was diverted—as if often is—by a storefront massage business. Checking my wristwatch, I calculated I had just enough time for a twenty-minute chair massage.

I settled onto the light gray vinyl chair and placed my face inside the cushioned headrest. The massage therapist introduced himself. "I'm Lee," he said. "But you can call me Sawbones."

He must have seen the cartoon question mark floating above my head in an imaginary white bubble—*"Sawbones?"*—for he went on to tell me about himself.

Digging his thumbs into the back of my neck, Sawbones explained that massage was a new line of work for him.

"Do you like it?" I asked, my words muffled by the cushioned face rest.

"Yes, ma'am," he said, revealing a slight rancher's drawl. "I get to meet interesting people, especially here at the airport. A few weeks ago, I massaged the lawyer for the Oklahoma City Bomber. He was on his way to his client's execution." Sawbones paused, as if remembering the occasion. "He was a little tense."

Although his comment demanded a sarcastic response, I couldn't think of one fast enough. Instead, I asked Sawbones if he worked only at the airport.

"No, ma'am. I also have an office by the Stock Show Complex."

"The Stock Show Complex?"

"Yes, ma'am. That's because I have another business. Custom cowboy hats."

The cartoon question mark reappeared. "*Cowboy hats?*"

"Yes, ma'am. I sell them at the Grizzly Rose, the country-western bar north of downtown."

I inhaled the rosemary scent of the massage oil and debated whether to prod Sawbones for more information. Since I was unlikely to meet another cowboy-hat-making-masseur in the near future, I asked him if his massage business was growing.

"Yes, ma'am. See, I do horses too."

"Horses?" I asked, feeling like I was being sucked down a conversational rabbit hole.

"Yes, ma'am. Horses like massage. They can get testy though."

"I'll bet." I pictured a blonde Palomino lying hooves up on a massage table.

As Sawbones kneaded my upper arms, he asked what I did for a living.

"I'm a writer," I said. Actually, I didn't say that, because just then, Sawbones' fingers pushed my head into the headrest making my answer sound more like "Imamiffer."

Sawbones was unfazed. "Really?" he exclaimed. "I'm a writer too!" He said this as if we were distant cousins meeting at a genealogy conference. "I write scripts!"

"Scripts?"

"Yes, ma'am. See, I also perform in Wild West Shows."

The rabbit hole was getting deeper by the second.

"What kinds of things are in your shows?"

"Shoot-outs. Stuff like that. I have a friend who looks like Abraham Lincoln. He's gonna be in our show tomorrow night."

Now, I've never been that great at history but I've never really pictured Abe Lincoln in a shoot-out, except, of course, for the incident at Ford's Theater. I was about to ask Sawbones how Abe figured into his act when he pulled my arms behind my back and away from my body as if dressing a chicken. "You sure got some knots under here," he said, poking underneath my shoulder blades. I began to comprehend the testiness of his equine clients.

Soon, our twenty minutes were up and Sawbones handed me his business card. "Massage," it read. "For Horses *and* Humans."

"Just for future reference," he added, "I also do home massage. It's only fifty bucks and I bring my own table, oil, and CDs." I accepted the card graciously even though I was fairly certain I'd never pay a man named Sawbones to tote oil and soft music into my house.

• • •

It's been a week since my encounter with the custom-cowboy-hat-making, wild-west-show-performing, horse-and-human massage therapist and I can't get him out of my mind.

Now, I know there are people who might find Sawbones a little lowbrow and unfocused. These people would assume Sawbones was a drifter who hadn't found his true calling. But to me, Sawbones is wise. He can work indoors or out. He works with his hands and his mind. He also has built-in job security. The bottom could fall out of the cowboy hat market and Sawbones would still make it in the world.

Furthermore, Sawbones has already figured out what many of us spend our entire careers learning: How important it is to try new things. "Ma'am," he said, "I do all these things because I promised myself I would never do the same boring thing all day long."

Many people I know have said this same thing to themselves at one time or another. But the difference between Sawbones and most people is that he is not afraid to tackle new challenges, even if those challenges involve tense attorneys and testy horses. So think about Sawbones the next time you're confronted with a new opportunity. Even if the job or project doesn't work out the way you expected, you might end up with good fodder for airport conversation.

❖

Restoration Hardware

Yesterday, I was sitting in my office happily trying to win my tenth computer solitaire game when I remembered an e-mail I had to send. (Never underestimate the value of wasting time as a prompt for more valuable endeavors.) I clicked open my e-mail program and noticed my entire address book had somehow been deleted. Thousands of contacts created over the course of many years had simply vanished. How could this be? It was a new computer.

I tried not to regard the empty address book as an indication of my utter unpopularity; a sign that I should give up the charade of being a vital, productive citizen. Instead, I did what any calm, methodical problem solver would do when faced with such an enormous data loss: I opened and closed and opened and closed the program thirty times to make sure the address file was really gone. It was.

My mind racing, I thought of all the people I would now not be able to reach: friends, family members, editors, students, clients, classmates, and those people I used to know in college who've somehow tracked me down and sent messages gleefully reminding me of the time I threw up in the bathroom during a Kenny Loggins concert.

Without e-mail, I would be cut adrift to bob alone on the cold digital seas of the Internet. My work, indeed my entire life, would stop functioning. And no, to answer your question, I had not backed up my data file. But thanks for asking.

In the midst of opening and closing the program, I recalled

something my brother-in-law had recently told me: that the operating system I use has a "restore" function that allows users to return the makeup of their computer's files and programs back to a particular point in time. In my case, a place in time when the address book was still intact.

The restore function was astonishingly easy to use, and within five minutes my address book was restored to its previous level of ego-stroking abundance. And so I got to thinking: What if we had a restore function for our lives? Think of the possibilities.

Cholesterol too high? Restore yourself back to the younger you who could eat cheeseburgers and french fries with enthusiastic, lip-smacking abandon.

Embarrass yourself at yesterday's team meeting? Restore your dignity by resetting the clock to eight a.m., just before you suggested the president was a Cheezit without realizing he'd walked into the room.

Like your hair better before you trimmed your own bangs and made yourself look like someone fresh from electro-shock therapy? Click back to the moment before you decided to go looking for the kitchen scissors.

The possibilities, really, are endless. I could have definitely used a restore function last weekend, for example.

My sister and her family joined Angela and me at a rented condominium in the mountains. The first day we spent a wondrous afternoon skiing in the sunshine. We have photos of our apple-cheeked smiles to prove it. In the photos, we're wearing bright ski parkas and looking very much like the vibrant, young, happy family we are. We're the perfect four-color cover shot for a ski industry brochure.

The next day, however, was an entirely different matter. It had snowed overnight: six, sloppy, springtime inches, and it was still snowing—sideways —in the morning. Despite this, the lift lines were so long that several mealtimes would pass between the moment we stepped in line and the time we actually sat, frozen and hungry, in the chair for the frigid ride to the top of the mountain. Upon reaching the top, we confronted a steep slope crowded with timid vacationers from the flatlands who were hugging pine trees and trying through sheer will to reverse the effects of gravity. We joined in, and immediately regretted our decision.

Angela fell, hit the back of her head on hard-packed snow, got up, and drove promptly back to Denver.

My brother-in-law fell, lost his lift ticket, and poked himself in the eye searching for lost goggles.

My niece threw up in the lift line.

My nephew whined everyone was slowing him down.

And I remembered why I didn't have children.

Mind you, this was a vacation we'd all been looking forward to for months. But by the second day, we were sprawled on various points of the icy mountain: whining, cold, and utterly exasperated.

How nice it would have been to click a button and restore ourselves to the day before, when—as our photo proves—we were joyful vacationers enjoying a joyous day.

But then I got to thinking: by restoring ourselves to an earlier time, could we have completely avoided the disastrous day that followed? Well, yes, I suppose we could have. We could have slept in, gone out to breakfast at some fabulous warm and cozy bistro, engaged in witty, stimulating conversation, and then returned to the condo to politely play games with one another.

"Oh, no, honey, you go first. Please."

"Great move, Sis. I never would have thought of that."

But then again, we could have just as easily slept in, fought over who should do the dishes, and gotten in a car accident on the way home.

I guess I like the idea of taking a different path and restoring myself back to some youthful, happier ideal. But in reality, I'm not sure it would work.

If my family hadn't had such a disastrous day skiing, we might not have appreciated the good day we did have. If I could turn back the clock to more youthful, healthier days, I'd probably start listening to loud music, fighting with my mother, and refusing to clean my room. And it's not a bad thing, necessarily, to realize that it's inappropriate to call the president a Cheezit.

So I guess I'll continue the forward momentum of my life and save the restore function for computer hard drives and lost e-mail addresses. And next time, I'll resist the urge to trim my bangs with kitchen scissors.

Forty-Three Things I Now Do That I Never Thought I'd Do

1. Pluck hair from my chin.
2. Refer to young people as "young people."
3. Read a book called *Eating for Acid Reflux*.
4. Discuss acid reflux while dining with friends.
5. Find conversation about acid reflux riveting.
6. Get ready to write the next item on a list and forget what it was.
7. Pat my stomach after a good meal.
8. Remember the forgotten list item and snap my fingers.
9. Be able to tell the difference between a Northern Flicker and a Black-Capped Chickadee.
10. Prattle on at dinner parties about the cute things my dog does.
11. Trim my toenails in hotel rooms and leave the clippings on the floor. (Note to self: Remember to pack nail clippers for upcoming trip to Las Vegas.)
12. Write notes to self.
13. Drink tea with names like *Sleepy Time* and *Smooth Move*.
14. Golf.
15. Wonder how my life would have been different had I been named Britney or Sigourney or Nicole…
16. Snore.
17. Or Bubbles or Hillary…
18. Watch a video called *Caring for Your New Leather Furniture*.

19. Watch a video called *Happy Baking With Your New Bread Machine.*
20. Spend fifteen minutes searching for eyeglasses before realizing I was wearing them.
21. Crossword puzzles.
22. Fart when I laugh.
23. Burp when I sneeze.
24. Cry when I see parades, or young children with ice cream, or puppies.
25. Nap.
26. Take classes to learn fencing, art appreciation, pie making, boxing, golf, and Italian.
27. Complain I don't have any interests.
28. Befriend a psychic, former prostitute, several lawyers, and a Jehovah's Witness.
29. Complain that my friends aren't interesting.
30. Complain.
31. Nap.
32. Take close-up photographs of flowers.
33. Use words like, "hormonal imbalance" and "nest egg."
34. Order salad dressing on the side.
35. Ask that my steak be cooked a "teensy bit more."
36. Ask the waiter if he can substitute broccoli for the potatoes because potatoes are just so fattening, and although he's too young to worry about such things now, he will when he gets to be my age.
37. Leave generous tips for overworked wait staff.
38. Watch the History Channel.
39. Fall asleep in front of the television.
40. Nap.
41. Nap.
42. Repeat myself.
43. Enjoy getting older.

I Hereby Resolve...

It's two days before Christmas and I'm starting to work on my New Year's resolutions. Now I know some people—and I'm not naming names—can put off this task until January first when they take ten minutes during halftime to recreate the same self-improvement list they've made every year. But not me. I need to make a long list of vital life-changing activities, narrow it down, let it breathe overnight, wonder what I was thinking, throw the list away, and start all over again. As you might imagine, this takes time.

So I'm in San Francisco visiting my family and it's seventy degrees outside. Because it's such a stellar day, I decide to craft my resolutions while enjoying a hike with my best friend, Dennis.

Dennis and I drive north across the Golden Gate Bridge to Mt. Tamalpais. We stop at a ranger station and ask the nice man in the green uniform where a good hike might be.

"Well," he says, pointing at a wooden map posted nearby, "this here's a pretty four-mile path that ends at the little town of Stinson Beach. There, you can do a little shopping before hiking back up."

"Pardon me, sir. Did you say shopping? *On a hike?*" Dennis glares at me.

(Resolution #1: Stop being so sarcastic.)

Dennis and I trek into the woods and he begins to tell me, in great detail, about all the unsolved murders that have taken place on Mt. Tamalpais. Hangings. Stabbings. Execution-style slayings. Is it my imagination or is Dennis enjoying this story?

169

(Resolution #2: Be nicer to Dennis next year.)

We emerge from the woods onto a sunny hillside from which we can see miles of bright blue coastline. Optimism returns. We're two happy people skipping down yellow grass in the sunshine. We're healthy and in the prime of our lives. We're the opening shot of a commercial for allergy medication.

(Resolution #3: See #1.)

We arrive at Stinson Beach an hour later. Walking into the town, Dennis squints into the sun and looks back toward Mt. Tam. "Looks like a long way up," he says, and I agree. I'm hot. And tired. And whiny.

(Resolution #4: No matter how good the Cabernet is, stop at one bottle the night before a hike.)

After promising each other we will never tell anyone what we are about to do, we search for a taxi to take us back up the mountain. There's none around.

We walk into a nearby post office and ask the nice post-man in the blue uniform where we might get a cab. The nice postman throws his head back and howls laugh-ter toward the ceiling. "You might get a cab from San Francisco to come here," he says, wiping the tears from his eyes. "But that'll cost ya an arm and a leg." I ask Dennis if the investigators working on the Mt. Tamalpais murders ever mentioned anything about a man in a blue uniform.

(Resolution #5: Order stamps by mail.)

We back away from the counter and bump into a woman holding a canvas, floral print shopping bag. "Do you two need a ride?" she asks.

We nod.

"Here," she says, grabbing a yellow change of address card and thrusting it toward us. "Make a sign. Someone'll pick you up in no time."

"You mean…hitchhike?" Dennis asks, his face looking as if

she's just asked him to strip naked and deliver the mail.

"Of course that's what she means," I say, as I grab the yellow card and write the name of the road where our car is parked. As I darken in the letters, I think how my mother would kill me if she knew.

We go outside, I hand Dennis the sign, and before his arm is fully extended a gray Toyota hatchback screeches to a halt beside us.

"Get in," shouts a thin women with long straight brown hair. She's not a day over twenty-five but her order is so command-ing Dennis and I do as we're told. I wriggle into the back seat and push aside file folders, empty water bottles, and several colorful hacky sack balls. "I'm Surya," she says. Surya steps on the gas and the car lurches forward.

Believing it's important to learn everything you can about a driver to whom who've just entrusted your life, I ask Surya what she does for living.

"I'm a counselor and performance artist," she explains. "I help people experience their truths through dance. Tonight, I'm performing in Santa Rosa."

"I see," I respond, though of course I don't see at all. "What will you be doing exactly?"

"I don't know yet," Surya confesses. "I won't know till I step on stage. I let the energy of the audience shape my movements. That way, my dance will be a truthful reflection of the collec-tive consciousness of those present. *Their* truths will become *my* truths which will become *our* truths."

(Resolution #6: Never hike in Marin County again.)
As Surya careens up the windy mountain road, she talks about her work and her passion. "You can just tell when someone's not in touch with their truths because the atmo-sphere around them smells like a big smelly fart."

(Resolution #7: Get in touch with your truths.)
"And you know what's most sad of all," Surya adds, as she

pulls up alongside our car. "Most people are so focused on what's wrong and what's lacking and what needs improving in their lives that they never stop to realize the blessings and wealth they do have. If more people realized how good their truths really are, they wouldn't worry so much about self-improvement. Their lives would be better naturally." She stops the car and turns to look at us. "Get it?"

We do. Or at least I do. Dennis is too busy thanking God we weren't picked up by an axe murderer. And as we drive across the bridge toward San Francisco, I make one final resolution for the year: Stop resolving to improve and be thankful for what you've already got, including people who can teach you things when you least expect it.

HIGHER GROUND

My mother and I are standing inside the women's restroom at San Francisco International Airport. Mom is garbed in one of her many lightweight, color-coordinated, wrinkle-free traveling outfits. I'm in jeans, and I'm watching her pour cool bottled water into two plastic juice glasses brought from home. When the glasses are full, she hands them to me and drops a round, white Airborne tablet into each one. The water fizzes and turns slightly orange. Mom explains that Airborne is a potent combination of vitamins that helps fend off germs on long flights. Mom worked in a hospital emergency room for thirty-five years. She knows her germs.

"I never go anywhere without my Airborne," she says. This is the third time she's said this in the last ten minutes.

Mom are I are innoculating ourselves inside the ladies room because in thirty minutes, barring any unexpected delays, we will embark on a fifteen hour flight from San Francisco to Beijing for a three-week, no-spouses, no-siblings tour of China. Just my mother. And me.

Actually, the trip was Mom's idea. She wants to cruise down the Yangtze River before the massive Three Gorges Dam project completely swallows the river, its soaring black rock canyons, and the historic cities along its banks. She's been to China before—she's been everywhere before—but wasn't able to see the river, and when she mentioned to my father that she'd like to return, his response was straight out of the "I'm Over Seventy and Don't Have To Do Anything I Don't Want To" handbook. "Have fun," he said, his thumb poised above

175

the television remote control. "Because I'm not going."

Thinking the trip might be a way for Mom and me to connect on a tender and more intimate level, the level that self-help books say mothers and daughters are supposed to connect on, I told her I would go.

Looking back, I believe I may have made this offer after several glasses of Chardonnay.

BEIJING

Day one. We're traveling in a small white bus: Mom, me, and twelve other tourists who've signed up for Uniworld's "Splendors of China" tour. We're weaving through Beijing's crowded streets to Tiananmen Square, the first stop on a day-long tour of the city.

Our guide, Leslie, a tall slim young man with crumbs at the corners of his lips, is reciting a litany of facts about Beijing. There are eleven million people here, he says, and roughly eight million bicycles. There are 108 embassies. And since China began to open its doors to world markets five years ago, fifty McDonald's restaurants have opened in the city, and there are plans to add fifty more in the next twelve months.

As he says this, our bus passes a bright new red-and-yellow McDonald's on a heavily trafficked street. "Look!" Mom says, pointing at the restaurant with a glossy red fingernail. "Isn't that amazing!" Her thin eyebrows are raised high above her gold-rim glasses as if she is truly dazzled by this sight. As if seeing McDonald's in the middle of a busy city is as wondrous as a finding a rare mongoose in Madagascar.

We continue our tour and Mom finds many, many things to be amazed about. The price of postcards is amazing. The size of Tiananmen Square is amazing. The number of cars in Beijing since her last visit is amazing. It starts to rain and that, amazingly enough, is also amazing to my mother. Never before in the history of recorded travel has the commonplace been given so much credit.

The Great Wall

Day four. The Great Wall of China stretches some four thousand miles over rolling green hills across the northern end of the country. Our tour group travels to a portion of the wall just forty miles outside of Beijing. As we pull into the parking lot, I'm startled to realize that the wall, at least in this section, is not the undulating peaceful wall depicted in travel brochures. Here, the wall climbs steeply, stair after stair, rising a thousand or maybe fifteen hundred feet before the steps end and the smooth concrete pathway begins. Although it's early morning, already the lower part of the wall is packed pillar to brick with tourists in bright sun hats.

Mom and I step off the bus and start to make our way toward the wall. She walks a few steps behind me because she's seventy-three and her pace has slowed, and because I'm forty and inconsiderate.

I walk up the first small set of stairs and turn to wait for her. The sun is warm, and after the gray, noisy congestion of Beijing, the peaceful green countryside is a welcome relief. I look down at my mother as she starts up the stairs. She's got short pale red hair that she keeps tightly permed because she doesn't like to fuss with it anymore. Her skin, which she's cared for with religious devotion for decades, is smooth for her age. But it's whiter than it used to be. And as I watch her making her way toward me, I realize it's not just her pace that's slowed. Her overall demeanor is more cautious. When did this happen?

Mom starts up the steps. A small black video camera is slung around her neck and she cradles it close to her chest with one arm. She rises one step and starts to approach the second when the tip of her tennis shoe catches the step's rough edge and she falls, swiftly and without warning, to the ground. Her video camera hits the pavement with a metallic thud.

Startled, I rush back down the stairs.

"Are you okay?" I ask.

"I can't believe I fell," she says. "One minute I'm standing, the next minute I'm on the ground." She chuckles, but I sense the laugh may be for my benefit. I help her up and she sits unsteadily on a low concrete rise nearby. She wipes dust from the knees of her royal blue pants. Her face is flushed, but whether it's from the heat or embarrassment or worry it's hard to tell.

"Did you hurt yourself?"

"Oh, no. I'm fine. Just clumsy. I don't do well with stairs anymore. You go ahead, honey."

I glance sideways at the wall and feel myself stretched in painfully opposite directions like some crazy cartoon cat: my aging mother tugging on one arm, a selfish little girl yanking on the other. I want to climb the wall, but...

Another member of our tour group saw Mom fall and she comes over to tell me she will sit with her.

"Really?" I ask.

"Of course," she says. She's about the same age as my mother.

"*Neither* of you needs to sit with me," Mom says. "I'm perfectly fine waiting here by myself. You go ahead."

And so I begin to climb the hard stone steps. One by one, up and up and up, past bundles of German and Japanese and Spanish tourists. I feel tense, like I shouldn't be here, but the views of the jagged green hillside are so stupendous I begin to relax. I stop, look at the hazy horizon and thank God for the ability to travel to such awe-inspiring places. I climb some more and stop again, this time because I realize I've just spoken to God, something that's completely out of character for me. But I'm on the Great Wall and, well, if you can't speak to God here where can you? And so I continue...to climb...to inhale the experience...and to thank God for the life I've been given. But in between these tentative entry-level prayers of thanks, I'm also begging, *begging*, God to keep my mother healthy and promising, *promising*, that if he does I will be kinder and more forgiving during those times when my mother repeats herself, makes inane comments, or otherwise dares to be herself as opposed to my thoroughly unattainable Hollywood ideal of what a mother should be.

Ninety minutes later I rejoin my mother and the other travelers on the bus. I sit down next to Mom, who seems to have recovered just fine, and she begins telling everyone about her fall. "Just call me Clumsy Betty," she says. Someone in bus chuckles at the Clumsy Betty comment and this serves to encourage her. She repeats the story, dialing up the volume and adding little embellishments for each new person to arrive.

"And then Clumsy Betty fell on the second step..."

"So then Clumsy Betty waited for her daughter at the bottom..."

"That's just me, Clumsy Betty."

I'm not sure, but I think God is testing me.

PACKING

Day five. Tomorrow morning, we'll be flying south to Xian on our way toward the Yangtze River. Mom and I are in our dimly lit hotel room and she's repacking her suitcase. Unlike me, my mother is an organized traveler who believes if you've got one small travel bag for your clean underwear, and one small travel bag for your dirty underwear, why not allocate small travel bags for everything in your suitcase, including socks, shoes, film, clothespins, make-up, shampoo, pens and pencils, books, medicine, camera, slippers, evening wear, day wear, sunglasses, passport, jewelry, and hair dryer.

Her travel bags are not all alike, however. She utilizes satchels, duffels, cubes, totes, containers, pouches, jewelry kits, toiletry kits, camera kits, and other specially designed, one-of-a-kind, perfect-for-just-this-one-item travel receptacle all of which are placed, one inside the other, like an infinite succession of Russian nesting dolls.

Mom has been zipping and unzipping her satchels for the last hour and it appears she's organized herself to the point of paralysis. She can't seem to find anything, and in an admirable attempt at self-coaching she's been trying to talk herself through the process.

"Let's see now," she says. "Where did I put my makeup kit?" She reaches to the far end of her suitcase and peers inside an elastic pocket. "Nope. Not here. Hmmm." She steps back, drums her fingers on her lips, and makes that absent-minded clicking sound with her tongue that she's doing ever since I can remember.

"Maybe it's here under my nightgown." Click. "Nope." Click. "Not here." Click. Click. She snaps her fingers. "Now I remember! I left it in the bathroom. Okay. Now. Where's my film bag?"

I screw in my earplugs, turn over in bed, and attempt to sleep.

THE BIG OLD GOOSE PAGODA

Day six. We're standing in front of the Big Old Goose Pagoda, a Buddhist temple with seven stories signifying the seven steps to Nirvana. At the entrance to the temple, people are kneeling on colorful satin pillows and bowing with bouquets of smoky red incense. A tremendous gold statue of Buddha sits in front of the worshippers just inside the temple.

Watching them, I think about the Buddhist ideal of right mindfulness, of the need to let go of attachments whatever they might be—thoughts, embarrassments, annoyances. I think how much more content I would be if only I could embrace the Buddhist ideal of living fully in the present. But while I'm thinking about Buddhism, I'm also thinking about my mother and I'm thinking about our trip and I'm thinking that perhaps I've been a bit impatient with her. After all, she's never interfered in my life. Never made me feel guilty for not coming home at Easter. Never judged the choices I've made in clothing or relationships or jobs, and I've made hideous judgment-worthy choices in every category. I'm thinking about all of this as I step onto a smooth slanted piece of concrete. My sandals, which have flat, well-worn souls, don't have enough traction to hold me upright and I fall, swiftly and without warning, to the ground. My camera, which is slung around my neck, hits the pavement with a metallic thud.

ALL ABOARD

Day seven. A third of the trip has passed and we're making our way down the steep concrete ramp that will take us onto the Victoria Princess, the small cruise ship that will be our home on the Yangtze River for the next week. Mom's worried about being able to make it down the ramp with her bad hip, so I lug her carry-on suitcase and mine, while she grabs the elbows of two Chinese ship workers. Slowly, she inches her way down the steep ramp toward the boat, bookended by the two young men in their identical white waist coasts.

Me, I'm starting to suffer all-inclusive tour fatigue. I'm not used to guided tours and published daily schedules and little red-and-white Uniworld flags and the need to make polite conversation at breakfast with people whom you've spent every waking hour with for days. Although you ask, you really don't care how well they slept the night before. Not really. Not one teensy bit. I acquired my travel legs twenty years ago backpacking through Europe without an itinerary or return ticket home. In the intervening years, I've managed to decide which country to visit, how to get there, where to sleep and eat, and what sights to see without the help, thank you very much, of a detailed itinerary (complete with shopping opportunities!) slipped under my hotel room door each night.

I reach the ship's entrance and turn around to watch my mother in her stark white Reebok athletic shoes, baby-step her way down the ramp. She's long retired, slightly overweight, concerned about her hip, and walking with the aid of not one but two escorts. And yet, she's smiling. It's a calm, beatific, take-the-moment-in-and-savor-it-while-it-lasts smile. She's Miss America displaying her tiara to the crowd. Queen Elizabeth waving from the balcony at Buckingham Palace. And for some reason this irritates me even further. She reaches the ship's entrance and turns to her young escorts.

"It's been a long time since two handsome young men escorted me anywhere," she says. They nod and bow vigorously. It's clear they haven't a clue what she just said.

ON THE RIVER

Day nine. We've been cruising down the Yangtze River for two days and I'm feeling more relaxed. The boat's gentle rocking and the long stretches of time available for reading have allowed me to settle into my role as traveler, my mother my constant companion.

At present, we're sitting together on the ship's windy deck and Mom is telling me for the second time today that there are 109 tourists on board the small ship.

"I know Mom," I say. "Leslie told us that yesterday."

"I just find it so fascinating. Most of the ships I've been on are so much larger."

"I know Mom," I say.

She's quiet for a moment. The briefest of moments.

"Did you know the captain has sixteen years of experience?" she asks.

"You mentioned that."

My mother embraces details like this, collecting them like tiny shells on a beach, as if together they might create something grand or at least suitable for a bathroom decoration. She routinely reports the exact time, every morning, when our daily schedule arrives. She monitors the temperature fluctuation in our room. And, as if hired by the cruise line to monitor the crew's efficiency, she gleefully announces when our scheduled day trips actually depart as opposed to the time they were scheduled to depart.

"Why do you care, Mom?" I asked yesterday, when she pointed out that our shore excursion to a nearby temple lasted thirty minutes longer than scheduled.

"I just find it interesting."

I look at the misty riverbanks as our ship glides by. Over the last two days, we've disembarked periodically to visit a village or museum or temple, all of which will be murkily submerged when the Three Gorges Dam—China's most ambitious construction project since the Great Wall—is complete, and the natural course of the flowing green river abruptly ceases. Seven years from now, the jumble of houses and schools and factories that line the riverbanks will be nothing more than quiet underwater ghost cities. Altogether, two million people will be displaced by the rising water, most of them to be relocated by the government to the tall concrete apartment buildings being constructed high on the hillsides.

Perhaps my view is naïve, that of a tourist with limited information, but I sense the Chinese people who live here are utterly resigned to their fate; resigned to losing their pagoda-roofed homes, their goldfish ponds, and the craggy rocks where they've fished with children and grandchildren for generations. Here, perhaps more than anywhere else, time flows with the river. People seem to understand that the only way to adapt to the distressing changes wrought by time is to move—willingly or not—to higher ground.

SAMPAN

Halfway through our trip. Today, we'll be traveling by sampan up the Danang River, a narrow winding tributary of the Yangtze. To get there, we must leave the ship, hike up a muddy hillside, and board a bus that will take us through a small windy town to the river.

We disembark from the Victoria Princess and are greeted by beggars: a blind young boy with milky, blue-gray eyes rolling in opposite directions; a fully grown man with horribly misshapen baby legs; another man holding a grimy plastic bowl between two handless arm stumps, a disfigurement that looks less genetic than cruelly intentional.

I link my right arm under Mom's left arm and she grabs my

hand for balance. We pass the beggars and start up the muddy path toward the top of the hill. Thin red strips of carpet have been laid at various points on the path to make walking easier, but it's raining steadily, if lightly, and the carpet strips are soaked through. The air smells like damp grass and rotting fish and diesel exhaust.

Slowly, Mom and I make our way up the riverbank, stopping to make sure each step lands on firm earth. Mom is gripping my right hand so tightly the backs of her knuckles are white. Halfway to the top, it starts raining more heavily, and we stop to retrieve the umbrellas in my backpack. I open them and hand one to Mom. Her round pink face is shiny wet from the rain. She hugs the umbrella close to her body, grabs my arm again for balance, and we continue our slow, step-by-step ascent, looking down at our feet the entire way. Most of our group has already reached the bus.

My stomach's knotting with acid worry. I'm worried about the rain. I'm worried about getting up the mountain. I'm worried about getting back down the mountain, and I'm just about to suggest we nix this trip and return to the boat, when my mother stops and looks up at me, her shoulders bunched up like a little girl's with secret news to share. "Isn't this exciting!" she says.

Startled, I look over at her. Her bright open expression tells me she's not kidding. She really does believe this is exciting. Her comment is so unexpected and so genuinely honest that I almost begin to sob out of sheer relief and admiration. The lenses of her glasses are fogging up. Her white shoes are dirty. She has half a hillside still to climb—bad hip and all—and she's having a jolly good time of it. If she were not already my mother, at this very moment I would desperately want her to be. She's no longer the aging mother I have to worry about; she's the cool mom who makes the most perfect sandwiches on the block.

We reach the top of the hill, ride the bus to the sampan—a creaky, flat-bottom boat with used airplane seats and open-air windows—and begin our afternoon's journey along the green river. The sampan stops for lunch, and several people get off to eat boxed lunches on shore. But Mom and I stay behind, and after eating our own lunches, we make our way to the restroom at the back of the sampan. The bathroom contains a single filthy, hole-in-the-floor toilet, the kind prissy Westerners like us aren't used to. There are no curtains on the rain-splattered window. No toilet paper on the roll. The door doesn't shut. Mom hands me some tissue from her fanny pack and stands guard at the door while I go inside. We then switch places and I guard the door for her.

Afterward, sitting back in our seats, I ask my mother whether she thinks any of my three sisters would want to do this trip. "You know," I say. "Climbing muddy hills, going into dirty bathrooms without seats."

Mom laughs. "What do you think?" she says, ever the diplomatic mother.

"I don't see anyone in our family doing this but us," I say. And then I raise my hand like a baseball player who's rounding home plate and getting ready to smack the palms of his excited teammates. Mom looks at my hand with her hazel eyes, the eyes that are like my own. She then raises her hand and we slap them together in the air between us.

I'm not sure, but I think this is the first time I've ever high-fived my mother.

GUILIN

Day seventeen. In the last week, we've traveled through the Yangtze's towering gorges, visited national parks, and toured the dam's colossal construction site. We've visited silk rug factories, eaten shrimp dumplings, bought carved stone turtles, sipped tea at teahouses, and snapped a highly unnecessary amount of photos of pandas at a local zoo.

We're now in Guilin, a southern city surrounded by tall, emerald, up-and-down mountains, the kind of mountains pictured on every travel poster of China ever produced. The scenery here—the winding Li River, the flat green rice paddies, the mountains shrouded in mist—is so spectacular that if you're a landscape painter in China with any ambition at all, you head to Guilin.

We stop at an art school and visit its crowded sales gallery. Every space on every wall is taken by paintings and scrolls and calligraphy. I immediately spot a painting I want, but the price—$4000 U.S.—is more than I can afford. The salesperson, a short young man in a pink shirt, offers to negotiate. Within seconds, we go from $4000 to $2000 to $1500 to $1200. I tell him I can only afford $300. He walks away.

Thus schooled in the art of Chinese negotiation, I find another set of paintings. They are seasonal landscapes: one an energetic green summerscape; the other, a peaceful tan-and-orange painting of the river in fall. The artist, I learn, is a professor at the school.

The short man in the pink shirt returns. My mother joins us. He starts the negotiation at $500 for each painting. I shake my head. My mother shakes her head. The price drops to $400.

"No thank you," I say and start to walk away. This isn't a tactic; I really don't want the paintings that badly.

"Offer him less," Mom whispers to me, while poking me gently in the side. And then I remember: Mom is nothing if not a deal-driven shopper. She's been known on several occasions to combine newspaper coupons, senior discounts, and credit-card rebates to create a trifecta of price discounts during a single department store transaction.

And so I resume negotiations. And soon, I'm wanting the paintings like a child wants presents. But I deftly manage to keep my cool.

"Four hundred," he says. I shake my head.

"Three hundred," he says. I frown.

"How about two hundred," I say. "For both."

The man in the pink shirt scowls.

"He's mad," Mom whispers. "That's good. See if he'll go any further."

And so I ask him to throw in a hardback coffee table book of the artist's work.

"Must check wit mann-ger," he says, and walks out of the gallery into some hidden back room.

Mom is beaming. *Beaming*.

The man in the pink shirt returns and we agree on $265. But when he rings up the purchase, it's clear he thought I only wanted one.

"No," I tell him, "$265 for *both*."

Now he's really steamed, and he marches back to speak with the mann-ger once again. We wait by the counter. Mom is as excited as I've even seen her. Any moment now, I expect her to start barking, clapping her hands, and rolling around on the floor like some crazy carnival seal.

The man returns and without uttering a word wraps up the second painting and the book and hands me all three purchases for $265.

Mom and I return to the hotel where I'm immediately struck with buyer's remorse. I chide myself for getting seduced by the bargaining. I wonder where the heck I'm going to hang two Chinese landscape paintings in my decidedly un-oriental Colorado home. But when my mother starts telling our travel companions about my extraordinary negotiating prowess, I forgive myself for getting carried away.

Suddenly, two hundred and sixty-five bucks seems like a small price to pay for a mother's adoration.

CALLING HOME

Day nineteen. My family operates under a strict code of conduct where problems with family members are concerned. The code goes something like this:

1. Never speak directly to another family member about a problem involving said family member.

2. Instead, tell a sister about the problem and swear her to secrecy.

3. Sit back, relax, and know that by having talked to a sister, word of the problem will eventually travel to its necessary target.

Two days after our art negotiations, I call home and learn via Angela who's talked to Debbie who's talked to my father that my father is desperately missing my mother. We've been gone more than two weeks, and it's the longest separation my parents have endured in more than fifty-three years of marriage.

I tell my mother Dad's missing her.

"Really?" she asks, her voice softening. "He *misses* me?"

"Yes," I tell her. "Debbie said he's really struggling without you."

"*Struggling?*" she says. "Wow." All at once, she looks bewildered and pleased and uncertain, as if she's just been given the gift of magic for one day and is not quite sure what to do with it. And then she gets a bit giddy.

"I think I'll give him a call!" she says.

I get into the shower to give her privacy. And as I wait for the water to warm up, I think about how people can surprise you. Even people you've known forever.

HONG KONG

Day twenty. After the brown and crumble and haze that is mainland China, Hong Kong's crisp glass and steel skyscrapers and penetrating blue sky inject us with a burst of renewed travel energy. Feeling celebratory and closer to home, Mom and I spend our last day of vacation doing what one does in Hong Kong: shopping.

We take the Star Ferry across the harbor to Kowloon and buy cashmere sweaters, jade bowls, knock-off watches, and opium pipes. We visit a jewelry store and allow a short woman behind a long glass counter to talk us into two identical gold necklaces, one for "mama" as the sales clerk calls her, and one for me.

That night, we meet the last remaining members of our tour group for a farewell dinner at a swank restaurant on the top floor of our hotel. The restaurant's long windows overlook the harbor and we watch the sun set over the water and the night-lights rise on the buildings. Our meal is extraordinary: heavy silver, thick linen napkins, and a seemingly endless succession of shrimp, spring rolls, chicken satay, halibut, lobster, several gooey, perfect, desserts, and lots of wine. I buy my mother dinner, and in the elevator on the way back to our room, she thanks me.

"Oh, honey," she says. "I felt so special dining in such an elegant place. I'm not used to that kind of treatment." The elevator opens and I step aside to let her exit. That's too bad, I think to myself. She deserves that kind of treatment.

We walk into our hotel room and Mom spends the next hour repacking for the long international flight home. She's just about through when she remembers her Airborne, and spends another fifteen minutes digging through her satchels for the fizzy vitamins and two plastic juice glasses.

Once found, she holds the small tube of Airborne triumphantly in the air. "I never go anywhere without my Airborne," she says.

"I know, Mom," I say, smiling at her across the room. "I know."

ACKNOWLEDGEMENTS

I want to express my sincere and lasting thanks to Angela Ekker, who continues to make blue bluer every day; Andrea Dupree, Michael Henry and the whole wonderfully supportive Lighthouse community; Janet Wiscombe and Carroll Lachnet, who graciously gave me the freedom to write personal stories in a business magazine; Chris Ransick, a wise friend and unofficial agent; Sonya Unrein and Matt Davis, for their vision and support; and, most especially, Allan Halcrow, who first encouraged me to find my voice, and, now that I've found it, still has the strength to take my phone calls.

ABOUT THE AUTHOR

Shari Caudron is a veteran freelance writer and columnist whose work has appeared in *Reader's Digest, Christian Science Monitor, Sunset Magazine, Workforce Magazine,* and many other publications. She currently teaches creative writing in Denver, Colorado.

Printed in the United States
115183LV00002B/18/A